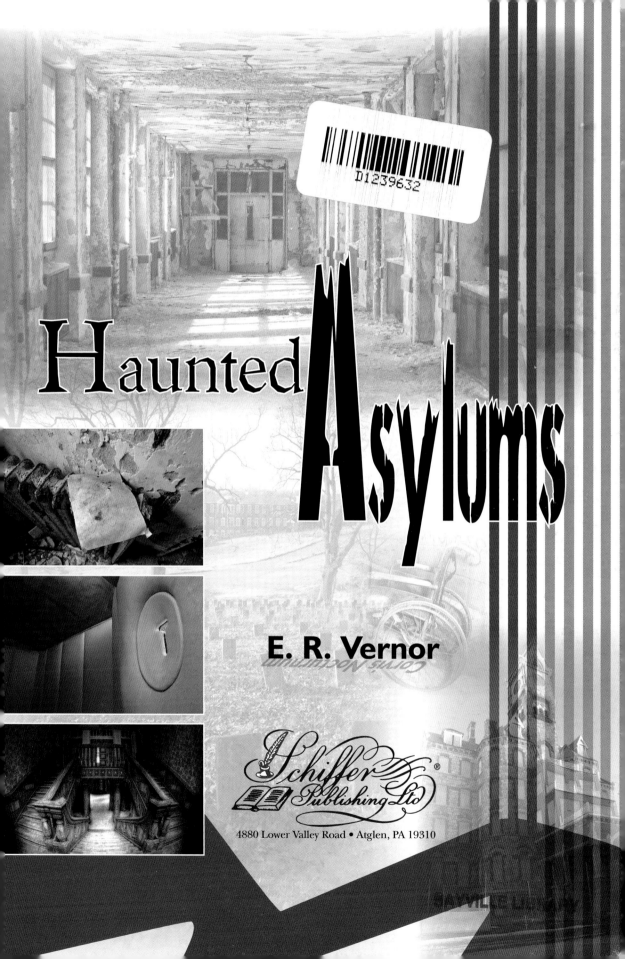

Haunted Asylums

E. R. Vernor

Schiffer Publishing Ltd

4880 Lower Valley Road • Atglen, PA 19310

Dedication

† In memory of family and friends who have passed on, especially my grandmother, who loved the occult, the paranormal, and all of the creative arts.

† A very special thanks to Tim Shaw, who was kind enough to contribute the introduction, as well as being brave enough to have visited his share of these locations. You, sir, have been a good friend and a staunch supporter. I feel you to be a man of integrity and passion....a true role model for others in your field.

† To Starr, Jack, Michelle, Chris, and Joe — thank you for helping me make Dark Moon Press what it has become.

Acknowledgments

The author would like to thank the following people for their inspiration: for her enthusiasm in my work and efforts to help me with yet another project, my editor Dinah Roseberry; Pete Schiffer; Nan, Ken Schuler, Mark Davis, David Jagusiak, Wayne Overla, and Chandra for your photography; and to author and radio host, Ed Shanahan, for his permission to reprint his article contained within. All of you made the wonders of these places so much more real for those of us not fortunate enough to see them for ourselves. Also, a thank you to all the people I have met along my path — you have enriched my life.

DISCLAIMER: The author nor the publisher advocates breaking and entering of abandoned structures. Not only is it illegal, but it is also highly unsafe, as the old buildings present a huge safety risk. Rusty metal, broken glass, and asbestos and mold filled places have rotting materials that may collapse and harm the urban explorer. Many of the locations featured in this book provide guided tours. Always check a location's website for details, rules, and regulations – that way you will avoid problems with property owners and local authorities.

Other Schiffer Books by the Author:
Cemetery Gates, Death and Mourning Through the Ages,
978-0-7643-3787-1, $24.99
I. Lucifer: Exploring the Archetype and Origins of the Devil,
978-0-7643-3919-6, $19.99

Other Schiffer Books on Related Subjects:
Urban Atrophy, 978-0-7643-3738-3, $39.99

Designed by Mark David Bowyer
Type set in Berylium / Humanist521 BT

ISBN: 978-07643-4147-2
Printed in China

Published by Schiffer Publishing, Ltd.
4880 Lower Valley Road
Atglen, PA 19310
Phone: (610) 593-1777; Fax: (610) 593-2002
E-mail: Info@schifferbooks.com

For the largest selection of fine reference books on this and related subjects, please visit our website at:
www.schifferbooks.com.
You may also write for a free catalog.

This book may be purchased from the publisher.
Please try your bookstore first.

We are always looking for people to write books on new and related subjects.
If you have an idea for a book, please contact us at
proposals@schifferbooks.com

Schiffer Books are available at special discounts for bulk purchases for sales promotions or premiums. Special editions, including personalized covers, corporate imprints, and excerpts can be created in large quantities for special needs. For more information contact the publisher.

In Europe, Schiffer books are distributed by
Bushwood Books
6 Marksbury Ave.
Kew Gardens
Surrey TW9 4JF England
Phone: 44 (0) 20 8392 8585; Fax: 44 (0) 20 8392 9876
E-mail: info@bushwoodbooks.co.uk
Website: www.bushwoodbooks.co.uk

Contents

Foreword

By Tim Shaw
Author of *Haunted Buffalo*

I have walked many darkened corridors alone, where screams have become mere echoes lost in time. The deafening silence causes me to share the apprehension that was once felt by those who were sheltered there. Although brick and mortar may make up these buildings, they seem to vibrate and share their sorrowful tales with anyone who cares to listen. As I wander these places where so many haunted memories linger, I question how humanity could have ever been so cruel.

Throughout history, civilized society has searched for a way to shelter and care for the infirmed, poor, and itinerant. However, by definition the word "civilized" has been subjective and must be judged upon the time period in which it was used. What we in our own "modern society" may consider as "civilized" is a far cry from what was the norm of an earlier age.

We often discover that asylums were descended from the practice of hiding those "people" whom society deemed pariahs. Those abandoned by ashamed birth parents, victims of "mental incapacities," and other unfortunates were all equally thrust into a nightmarish world. These poor wretches often spent their lives chained to a dank cellar wall.

Over time, as villages and towns grew, the need for a centralized facility to house such "people" grew with them. Hospitals and sanitariums were sometimes little more than prisons where the forgotten became victims of physical abuse and were sometimes subjected to horrific experimental treatments. It was these environments that often proved to degrade the mental states of the patients to that of animals.

Who were these people? Some of these patients were placed in these facilities after a shocking medical diagnosis while others found their way to these places simply because they became destitute after one of the many plagues that swept through the unsanitary conditions of urban areas. The reasons may have been many, but the end result was the same.

Brutal therapies were often administered on a daily basis in many of these facilities. The use of cold water immersion, administering drugs to cause seizures, as well as the surgical removal of parts of the frontal lobes of the brain, referred to as lobotomies, became standard procedures. Also, let us not forget about the now outdated belief that eugenics programs and forced sterilization were needed to keep certain traits, considered inferior, from spreading throughout the population.

Living in the Western New York region, I had developed an early fascination with the Buffalo State Asylum for the Insane, better known as the Richardson Olmstead Complex. It became in my young mind a place of mystery and horror. After it closed in 1974, whispers began to be heard about what took place there and the souls who walk its debris-filled halls.

After many years of exploring abandoned ruins and discovering the forgotten souls of these stone megaliths, I can think of no better person than Corvis Nocturnum to examine and chronicle the sometimes macabre world of asylums. He comes to this study well equipped with the eye of a scholar, yet he also possesses a keen and devoted interest in the esoteric and sometimes dark worlds that lie hidden or ignored. It is through his perceptions that the reader shall still find beauty in the forgotten relics of a somewhat barbaric past. Corvis Nocturnum dares to explore what many wish to forget and unearths a reality that is sometimes unpalatable to the mundane world. That is what makes this study of asylums important and quite poignant for generations to come.

Introduction
The History of Mental Institutions

Prior to the year 1844, the mentally ill were stashed away in prisons or taken away, crammed into anywhere they could be kept out of sight from "decent folk," many times hidden in the basements of public buildings. Later on, special facilities were built to house them when overcrowding became an issue. Long before the advent of modern psychology, and psychoanalysis developed by Sigmund Freud and accompanying psychiatric drugs, far more than just the mentally ill were housed in these institutions known as sanatoriums or insane asylums. Wardens lumped all types together — hundreds to thousands of individuals — including epileptics, the homeless, imbeciles, habitual criminals, war veterans dealing with post-traumatic stress disorder, as well as the mentally insane. Bethlem Royal Hospital in London is the world's oldest facility that housed the mentally ill, as far back as 1357. Back in the eighteenth century, the public could pay a penny for the privilege of watching the "freaks," as they were called; this gave spectators the chance to poke the caged patients with a long pole. As an indication of what a house of horrors Bethlem Royal Hospital was, the word "bedlam" is derived from its name, but in the middle of the nineteenth century, reformers like Dorothea Dix, pushed to improve living conditions and treatment at the facility. Many of these institutions were originally treatment centers for diseases like alcoholism or tuberculosis; however, without federal regulations in place to maintain guidance, many developed sinister reputations for unspeakable neglect and cruelty.

Haunted Asylums will explore the horrendous past of more than fifty mental institutions. Accompanied by stories of alleged hauntings and amazing photographs, author E. R. Vernor provides a glimpse into a cold, empty, closed world, where "incurables" were sent as a last resort. With no expectation that they would ever return to society, many of them existed according to their ability to work and their manageability. Patients used as unpaid labor is what mental institutions across the country kept going at best and as living medical experiments at worst.

In the mid-nineteenth century, Dr. Thomas Story Kirkbride, an influential psychiatrist who served the Pennsylvania Hospital as the superintendent from 1841 to 1883, became famous for creating a humane and compassionate environment for his patients. Dr. Kirkbride influenced how mental hospitals were to be built for years with his book *On the Construction, Organization and General Arrangements of Hospitals for the Insane*, which was published in 1854. The mentally ill were no longer kept like animals as they often were in the years before the Kirkbride model. This reformer believed that beautiful settings restored patients to a more natural "balance of the senses." Dr. Kirkbride's progressive therapies, innovative writings on hospital design, and guidelines for staff management became known as the "Kirkbride Plan," which influenced, in one form or another, almost every American state hospital to improve circumstances for the mentally insane. Kirkbride's design involved segregating the patients by sex and degrees of illness — the worst, or most insane, were to be kept in the furthest quarters, away from the better patients and preventing them from escaping. The vast majority of institutions of this type was designed with long infirmary wings that extended off the towering administration building and was dubbed the "bat-wing" design, which meant that there was a main center in each building and then the wings extended right and left, and then angled again so that they ran slightly backward...like a bat's wings. These majestic buildings are your classic haunted buildings we often see in such horror films as *The House on Haunted Hill* and *Session Nine*, among others that depict insane asylums.

The mere size and atmosphere of the buildings bring to mind these kinds of images. The architecture's foreboding Gothic aesthetic alone will unnerve the visitor even today, but it runs deeper than that. When one considers, for example, these decaying hospitals' former use of less than moral practices, it becomes clear that truth is more unsettling than fiction. In the early years of psychiatric institutionalization, mentally ill patients were subjected to unorthodox cruel treatment and restraints that were said to function as "cures," but were really nothing more than Nazi-styled medical experimentation. For example, state institutions in 1923 saw the birth of the Board of Eugenics, which allowed for the "sterilization of all feeble-minded, insane, epileptics, habitual criminals, moral degenerates, and sexual perverts who are a menace to society." The board reasoned that the gene pool would be stronger if what they termed defective patients were not allowed to breed. As such, sterilization was used as a condition of release from state institutions or as punishment. A total of 65,000 forced sterilizations were performed in the country from 1917 to when the board was finally abolished in 1983. This practice was aided by funding from wealthy American business tycoons such as John D. Rockefeller and Andrew Carnegie in the 1920s.

Other barbaric treatments, including patients being confined in restraining devices, solitary confinement, beatings by both brutal wardens and violent inmates, electroshock therapy, untested drug experimentation, and lobotomies, were performed until the 1970s. Electroconvulsive therapy (ECT) is a procedure in which electric currents are passed through the brain, deliberately triggering a brief seizure to cause changes in brain chemistry that can immediately reverse symptoms of certain mental illnesses. Sadly, my research shows that even today, in the U.S. alone, more than 100,000 people are electro-shocked every year, the majority of them elderly. According to the Mayo Clinic, the side effects experienced can include confusion, memory loss, nausea, vomiting, headache, jaw pain, and muscle aches or spasms. The FDA, explaining that the treatment has so little efficacy and is so obviously damaging — it routinely produces an acute state of delirium and confusion with severe memory loss — said it should be banned in a document that has now been published in many scientific journals. The writings of Dr. Peter Breggin on ECT can be found in *Brain-Disabling Treatments in Psychiatry: Drugs, ECT, and the Psychopharmaceutical Complex, Second Edition* (2008).

Asylums at this time were more often than not a facade for mental abuse and torture. In the book *Madhouse: A Tragic Tale of Megalomania and Modern Medicine*, author Andrew Scull wrote about the appalling career of Dr. Henry Cotton, superintendent of the Trenton, New Jersey, hospital for the insane in the beginning of the 1900s and how he would extract or amputate any part of the body he felt might be causing the mental issue. The operations were performed without knowledge of the procedure or consent of the patient.

Since ancient Greece and Roman times, another method of boring holes into the skulls of mental patients, known as trepanning, was practiced for a variety of conditions, including headaches, insanity, and delusions. Still others in Europe believed that insanity was caused by abnormal blood flow. As you will see in the photos of this book, many of the locations had density chairs and glass jars of teeth, due to the fact it was thought removing them would provide a cure. Also, more of my investigating led to the discovery that inmates were subjected to excessive bloodletting, spinning chairs, and gyrators.

"Insane teeth." *Courtesy Ken Shuler.*

Another widespread treatment used by centers in the United States and parts of the United Kingdom was hydrotherapy, which used water to treat symptoms. In mental hospitals, it was used to treat psychiatric symptoms by soaking the patient in a warm bath because it was thought to have calming effects. Other similar styled versions used to calm them was to place a patient in a bath of running cool water over pulse points, such as the wrists and ankles; this was believed to lower the body temperature, calm nerves, and slow the pulse rate. This was only good for the symptom treatment at best; at worst it was abused as a deterrent, as you can see in the photo of the tubs in the Norwich and Grafton facility, where rows of cast iron tubs had straightjacket styled covers bolted over them *(see next page)*.

Insulin coma therapy (ICT) was a form of psychiatric treatment in which patients were repeatedly injected with large doses of insulin in order to induce comas for weeks; this method was used extensively in the 1940s and 1950s, until it was replaced by psychiatric drugs.

To quote one of my photographers, Ken, who braved more than a few treacherous places, "In what ways we treat our mentally ill speaks volumes about our society as a whole." You will see through their eyes what remains of these buildings; their sad conditions and items left behind are terrifying in what it reveals about the treatment those poor souls once went through there.

During the 1970s and into the 1980s, a great deal of these old sanatoriums closed. The warehousing of patients in these gigantic, cold institutions began to be used less and less, as patients' rights advocates believed that the mentally ill could be rehabilitated and lead normal lives with more effective psychiatric drugs. One such drug was Torazine, pioneered in 1954; in the 1970s, new drugs were given to juvenile delinquents, the elderly in nursing homes, and nearly half of the nation's "mentally retarded" patients, who called it chemical straightjackets or, more commonly, "zombie juice." It was also during this period that Valium became the most prescribed drug in America, as pharmaceutical corporations increased more anti-depressant medications, including Prozac, which soon followed during the 1980s.

As decades passed, the buildings remained silent, packed with vast amounts of patients' old psychiatric evaluation records that were left behind to gather dust and mold, both of which has formed in these forgotten dank basements. According to those who have been brave enough to explore these places, the storage rooms are full with floor to ceiling file cabinets holding clinical analyses regarding patient's drawings and medical records, holding clues to their lives and the procedures they endured. These records documented thousands of people's lives at the hospital — from the time of admission to their burial — marked by only their patient number on the grounds of the place they were condemned to live and die.

Grafton State Hospital. *Courtesy of Nan Guzauski.*

They say that a picture is worth a thousand words and that may very well be true. If you know what I have come to know about the ugly history of psychiatric progress of mental patients, then the horrific details mentioned earlier become even more chilling as you see the empty and forlorn remains of these facilities, whose floors have rotted and caved-in to the depths. Many of them have collapsed walls and ceilings, are empty, and echo only animals' scurrying movements, forgotten until they are happened upon by what is known as the "urban explorer." These urban explorers took the photos for this book, risking their lives and arrest to trespass into these derelict structures. Today, these abandoned state institutions have been converted into other uses or remain in shambles, waiting to be sold. Many government officials want these vast unused parcels of property to be converted for several reasons, primarily for the value of the property and to rid themselves of potential liabilities. It is a shame that so many of these buildings, which have such a fascinating past, do not get restored as historical landmarks due to their significance, but instead become shopping malls and apartment complexes for wealthy developers.

Due to the severity of trauma that the decades' worth of emotionally disturbed inmates experienced, both from their own mental afflictions and forced treatments over the course of their lives prior to their death, paranormal investigators and psychic mediums believe that these former patients have left specific imprints of intense thought and emotional energy within these buildings' walls, leaving the places forever haunted. The residual impressions of the past would certainly be strong in a building where mentally ill people were housed and where, if provable, such psychic disturbances would be common. Hospitals have long been places where the spirits of the dead are said to linger. Are there actually lost and anguished souls trapped within these abandoned buildings? Are they truly the personalities of those who once lived in agony and despair? Or are these feelings simply those of the visitors, projected by the idea of spooky places due to films and campfire tales? The atmosphere of these places alone is more than enough to justify the reports of the apparitions and strange tales of ghostly encounters. I leave it up to you, my reader, to decide as I showcase these locations that stood out to me in my quest.

In *Haunted Asylums*, we will explore the history behind the infamous Riverside patient Mary Mallon, also known as "Typhoid Mary"; the sordid past of many notorious hospitals and infirmaries, including Danvers State Hospital in Danvers, Massachusetts, whose Gothic and foreboding buildings became both the inspiration and filming location for the movie *Session Nine*, and the Oregon State Hospital, where Jack Nicholson's famous *One Flew Over the Cuckoo's Nest* was filmed. So deeply felt to this day is the eerie vibe of such locations, movies continue to be made about them. While gathering information for this book, I happened to see the movie *Shutter Island*, in which a resident of a mental asylum goes missing and a U.S. Marshall, played by Leonardo DiCaprio, faces off against the facility's head psychologist, played by Ben Kingsley.

If such hauntings really and truly are the residual effects of trauma being imprinted on the final locations of one's life, then certainly such places where terror and insanity were commonplace would be the place for lingering spirits to remain, lost and wandering for eternity. Come, explore the most reputedly haunted asylums with me all the world over. *If you dare…*

Unknown asylum. *Courtesy Chandra Lampriech*.

The Asylums:
Haunted or Not?

When the Athens Lunatic Asylum in Athens, Ohio, opened its doors in 1874, many of its first patients were Civil War veterans suffering from post traumatic stress disorder. Athens Mental Health Center, also known as The Ridges, was originally called the Athens Asylum for the Criminally Insane. The State and Federal Government had purchased over 1,000 acres of land from the Coates family, whose farm had previously occupied the land. The main building, enormous in structure, was designed around the idea that it was therapeutic for patients to be housed in a facility that resembled a home. The less disturbed patients were housed closer to the center, where the administrative offices and employee housing were. The more violent patients were housed at the far end of the wings, away from employee housing and convenient exit and entry routes. The building housed over two hundred patients until overcrowding ensued in the early 1900s. The patient count then rose to nearly 2,000 patients in a building with only 544 rooms. The increases in population led to the decline of patient treatment. Once unique in its mental practices, the facility eventually fell prone to hostile patient care, including physical abuse, water treatment, shock therapy, and lobotomies. Today, Ohio University has converted the main building into a museum and offices, while the other buildings have long since been demolished.

Paranormal activity at this haunted insane asylum centers on the death of one patient — a woman named Margaret Schilling. On December 1, 1978, Margaret disappeared from one of the active wards. Workers found her corpse on the top floor of the ward, N. 20, which had been abandoned for years. The room was locked from the inside, and Margaret's body was nude. She had been dead for several weeks, as her body was not found for more than a month later. The official cause of death was heart failure, due to her exposure to the December cold in an unheated section of the hospital. The most common theory is that Margaret locked herself in the room to hide from nurses. However, questions surrounding her death remain a mystery to this day. If she called for help, why did no one respond? Why was she unclothed? Furthermore, why was her clothing laying neatly folded by her body? Once her body was removed, workers cleaned the room using very strong cleaning solvents on the cement floor, but the ghostly outline of her corpse always returns. By 1993, the Athens Asylum for the Criminally Insane closed its doors for good.

Bartonville Hospital

Bartonville Hospital is located on private property between the towns of Peoria and Pekin in Illinois. Construction on the first buildings began in 1885 and was completed in 1887. It was a foreboding structure bearing a strong resemblance to a medieval castle with battlements and turrets. Despite the huge costs involved in constructing it, the original facility was never used and was demolished, due to poor structural and design flaws. The hospital had been constructed over an abandoned coal mine and over time wide cracks appeared in the walls, believed to be caused by the collapsing of the old mine shafts.

In 1902, the hospital would reopen with Dr. George A. Zeller, a pioneer in mental health, as head administrator. The new hospital implemented what is known as the cottage system, consisting of no window bars or restraints, something that was unheard of in those days. The layout was unusual as well, consisting of thirty-three different buildings to house patients. There was also a nurse's home, domestic buildings where laundry was done, and a bakery and kitchen.

Dr. Zeller decided that deceased persons would be shipped home to their relatives, but that the asylum would take care of the burials of the unclaimed, which led to the creation of four cemeteries behind the main buildings. The older cemeteries are marked with stones that have only the patients' numbers because many of the patients came there without medical records or identification. The newer cemeteries had markers with the names, dates, and the patients' numbers on them. The oldest cemetery here would mark the location of the very first ghost story to be associated with the hospital. The director created a work detail to handle the burials of those who died during their time at Bartonville — the "undertakers" were both staff members and a half-dozen male patients.

While these men were in need of treatment, all of them were functional enough to do the job of digging and carrying the deceased to the grave. One of the most unusual men, according to Dr. Zeller, was a patient who was simply known as "A. Bookbinder." The man was a mute who had suffered a breakdown and his mental illness had left him incapable of coherent speech, so nobody knew his real name. Previously he had been working in a printing house. A Chicago officer who had taken him into custody wrote in his report that the man had been employed as "a bookbinder"; a court clerk listed this as the man's name and he was sent to the hospital as such. The doctor described the man as being strong and healthy, although completely uncommunicative, so the attendants enlisted him to assist in the burials of dead patients. "Old Book," as he began to be called, was especially suited to the work. Ordinarily, when the coffin was being lowered, the grave-diggers would stand back out of the way and wait silently for the funeral to end. At that point, they would set to filling the grave. Nearly every single patient at the hospital was a stranger and unknown to the staff, so the funeral services were mainly done out of respect, not out of any attachment to the deceased. Because of this, everyone was a little surprised when, at his first interment, Old Book proceeded to remove his cap, wipe his eyes, and weep loudly for the patient who had died. At each service, he would first use his sleeve to wipe away tears and then he would walk over and lean against the old elm that stood in the center of the cemetery and begin sobbing loudly. This massive old tree, known as the "Graveyard Elm," had been standing for many decades. As the years passed, "Old Book" died. Word spread among the staff about his funeral; more than one hundred uniformed nurses attended, along with the male staff members and several hundred patients. Dr. Zeller officiated the funeral proceedings himself and gave the eulogy. Dr. Zeller wrote in his journal, "Just as the choir finished the last lines of 'Rock of Ages,' the men grasped the ropes, stooped forward, and with a powerful, muscular effort, prepared to lift the coffin, in order to permit the removal of the crossbeams and allow it to gently descend into the grave." At a given signal, they heaved away the ropes and, in an instant, all four men sprawled on their backs. Old Books' coffin, instead of falling hard from the weight, bounced into the air, as if it weighed nothing. The shocked nurses were said to have screamed, half of them fleeing and the other half coming closer to the grave to see what happened. "In the midst of the commotion," Dr. Zeller wrote, "a wailing voice was heard and every eye turned toward the Graveyard Elm whence it emanated. Every man and woman stood transfixed, for there, just as had always been the case, stood Old Book, weeping and moaning with an earnestness that out-rivaled anything he had ever shown before." After a few moments of this, Dr. Zeller called over some men to remove the lid of the coffin, as he was convinced that Old Book was not inside...it had to be a joke. The lid was lifted immediately and the wailing sound stopped. Inside the coffin lay Old Book. Legend says that every eye looked upon the body and then over to the Elm, where it stood alone.

"It was awful, but it was real," Dr. Zeller wrote. "I saw it; one hundred nurses saw it and three hundred spectators saw it."

Strange as that may have been, the story does not end there. In a few days, the Graveyard Elm mysteriously began to wither and die. In spite of efforts to save it, the tree died the next year. Later, after the dead limbs had dropped, workmen tried to remove the rest of the tree, but stopped working after the first cut of the axe because an "agonized, despairing cry of pain" came from the base of the tree. After that, Dr. Zeller thought that the tree should be burned. According to the workers, as soon as the flames started flicking at the tree, they quickly put them out, explaining to Dr. Zeller that they heard a sobbing and crying sound coming from it. "Today, Old Book's grave remains without headstone or monument," Dr. Zeller wrote, "but if anyone asks where he is, those of us in the know point with a shudder to the remains of the Graveyard Elm."

After the death of Dr. Zeller, the hospital remained in continuous use for many more years, as it added care facilities for children and tuberculosis patients. Bartonville Hospital finally closed in 1972 and remained mostly empty for a number of years. In the 1980s, it became the property of the bank again, when the buyer declared bankruptcy. The remaining hospital buildings' owners hope to convert the place into office space. It is private property and trespassers are not allowed.

However, former Marine and private investigator Rob Conover has visited the former hospital site multiple times in the past. He is known as a ghost researcher, appearing on local and international television programs on ghosts and the supernatural. Mr. Conover claims he ran into an unexplained force, which, among other things, refused to allow him to open doors. During another visit, an apparition appeared on videotape when he left a camera running in an abandoned corridor.

Buffalo State Psychiatric Hospital

Buffalo State Hospital. *Courtesy of Ken Schuler.*

At 400 Forest Avenue in Buffalo, New York, bordering Buffalo State College and Route 33, is the facility known as "the creepy mental institute with the tower." However, area students and residents refer to it as the H. H. Richardson Complex, with the vacant Buffalo State Psychiatric Hospital standing as a monument to Buffalo's past. Built in1871, the building, when opened in 1880, was known by a variety of names, including the Buffalo State Asylum for the Insane, H. H. Richardson Complex, Buffalo State Lunatic Asylum, and Buffalo Psychiatric Center. The architect for the buildings was Henry Hobson Richardson (1838-1886).

Generally regarded by architectural historians as the first of the three greatest American architects — the other two are Louis Sullivan and Frank Lloyd Wright — Richardson was appointed to design the state hospital in 1870 and given the opportunity to utilize his own style of architecture, which has become known as Richardsonian Romanesque. As with the Kirkbride style, patients were separated by sex and the most violent patients resided the furthest away from the administration at the ends of the wings. They were separated by curved connecting hallways. Towers, 185 feet tall and topped with copper roofs, contained large iron doors that could isolate the ward in the event of a fire. Rough sandstone was used as the primary building material, giving the building a very dark hue, until in 1876 budget issues forced the use of brick for the outer three wards. Richardson died nine years prior to the 1895 construction completion, at the age of forty-eight.

Robert Whitaker, a *Boston Globe* journalist, wrote in detail on the unethical psychiatric treatments in his book, *Mad Medicine*. A common but little talked about practice was eugenics, which is the systematic sterilization of the mentally ill to prevent the reproduction of their mentally deficient genes into any offspring. Whitaker wrote in *Mad Medicine*, "In the 1930s, patients in New York state hospitals died at five times the rate of the general population, and mortality rates were particularly high for young people twenty to twenty-four years old — the very group that eugenicists did not want to see breed."

Injecting schizophrenic patients with insulin to induce supposedly brain-awakening comas was another common practice, wrote Whitaker. "They were in fact now close to death, their brains so depleted of sugar that only the most primitive regions, like basic brain functions were left intact." Whitaker said that there is a connection. "People who are mentally disturbed, or any type of alteration to the human psyche, have a higher tendency to have supernatural abilities. They have higher functions of the unconscious mind. So, there is a greater tendency of hauntings with a place related to those types of people."

The Richardson Complex once housed thousands of patients, some of whom slept in the halls or outside since the occupancy exceeded the building's design. The brick wards on the east side of the complex were demolished in the 1960s, and Buffalo State Hospital was officially closed to the public and patients in 1974. Today, entering the hospital is not allowed, but those who have broken-in report they have seen medical devices and decaying hospital beds. Jackie Constantine, a Buffalo State College graduate, managed to break into the hospital with friends. As the group made their way into the hospital, the floor beneath them caved in, which forced everyone to run back down...all the way to the basement. "The walls were thick stone, it was really dark. When we saw a sign for the morgue, we fled." *The Haunted Film* (hauntedfilm.com), a project run by the Buffalo organization Friends of Endangered History, is a mysterious, first-hand account of the supernatural filmed inside the hospital. The short film consists of a series of clips depicting several paranormal "anomalies."

The Haunted Film was a project that started in 2003 when a man stayed overnight in order to capture images of the hospital's rapidly deteriorating state. When going through the hours of footage, his former wife noticed something strange. Upon first viewing, the film shows a chair in the middle of a dark hall, tunnels flanked with rows of pipes, and a tall wooden ladder extending upwards. The camera work is jumpy, but, after viewing it several times, the viewer will notice some strange occurrences. The gate swings open by itself and in one section it looks as if a shadowy figure passes by a darkened archway — it moves too quickly and smoothly to be human. The amateur ghost investigator didn't recall seeing anything unusual at the time, but, if he had, he claims he would "have had a heart attack." He's not alone in his reports, though. To this day, people claim to hear screaming and see shadow images in some of the windows as they walk by.

Now these buildings are included as part of the campus of the Buffalo Psychiatric Center and today, 125 years after their construction, the two medieval towers stand tall with imposing heights. Instead of tearing them down for newer buildings, they remain gated. They are also on the National Register of Historic Places. The city of Buffalo has memorialized them by lighting them at night and heavily patrolling the area. As one of my photographers informed me, Buffalo State Hospital is locked up as tight as a prison with motion detectors and IR video cameras.

Buffalo State Hospital. *Courtesy of Ken Schuler.*

Historic plaque at Buffalo State Hospital. *Courtesy of Ken Schuler.*

Buffalo State Hospital. *Courtesy Wayne Overla.*

Back view, Buffalo State Hospital. *Courtesy of Ken Schuler.*

Opposite page and above: Patient room and lounge area, Buffalo State Hospital.
Images courtesy of Nan Guzauski.

Broadview Developmental Center

Built in 1939 near Broadview Heights, the Broadview Developmental Center was a psychiatric hospital constructed under the Works Progress Administration as part of President Roosevelt's New Deal, where it functioned as a Veterans Administration Hospital until 1966 when it was sold to the state of Ohio. The center was then converted into a psychiatric hospital and remained open until 1993 when the hospital lost its funding. Originally, the institution was largely used to treat tuberculosis, but was later converted to a developmental center, catering to the mentally handicapped. The facility included a full cafeteria, kitchen, dental offices, a beauty shop, and a chapel. It used what is known as the cottage system of treatment: having small cottages on the property, where patients who required less direct supervision lived. The campus also had a separate area for children and maternity patients. A majority of the staff offices were off-campus. This was done to minimize contact between patients and the rest of the world, as well as to reduce the risk of spreading tuberculosis. Broadview was known for the ghost called the "Pink Lady," an apparition staff and residents said roamed the halls and is occasionally seen through the windows.

Streptomycin was discovered in 1946, the first major antibiotic break-through that proved to be a potent treatment for the once deadly and widespread contagion known as tuberculosis; as a result, the need for facilities, such as Broadview, began to lessen more and more. The federal government sold the facility to the state of Ohio in 1966 and the hospital was converted into a psychiatric institution for patients with mentally developmental handicaps. It served as such for nearly three decades.

The increasing availability of anti-depressants and other psychiatric drugs, the backlash against social welfare programs, political pressures, and a public outcry of unrest over the stories of the inhumane treatment practiced at many other psychiatric institutions of its time led to significant cuts in federal and state mental health spending. As a result, in 1933 the Broadview Developmental Center closed, becoming a victim of deinstitutionalization. With the abandonment came a large controversy: the majority of the former patients had no relatives to claim them, so the former patients were released into the community. Personal artifacts belonging to former staff and patients were left behind. The old building was full of numerous filing cabinets filled with patient records, vast amounts of medical and office equipment were left inside the building, and all records of their treatment, progress, and illness have been lost.

In 1995, Broadview Heights purchased the former Developmental Center from the state of Ohio and tore down many of the outer buildings to erect a new police station on the grounds. The main building was partially renovated and transformed into a community center with an indoor swimming pool and recreational facilities. The city plans to expand the campus both for the government offices and the recreation center.

In the meantime, other buildings have remained empty, except for the homeless vagrants and vandals. To prevent more destruction, the windows were boarded and the city constructed a chain-link fence to keep out would-be explorers, as well as the paranormal investigators who started coming to the place due to rumors that the facility was haunted by former patients.

Cane Hill Asylum

Cane Hill Asylum in Croydon, Greater London, opened in 1883; at its peak, it housed up to 2,000 patients. The main buildings were designed by Charles Henry Howell and displayed the Latin motto that translates into: "I bring relief to troubled minds." The imposing Victorian asylum remained untouched until the 1960s, when Health Minister Enoch Powell called for the closure of the asylum and, by 1991, it had closed all but its secure units. The asylum was heavily under-used by the time it was completely shut down. Arson attacks, coupled with structural damage from the elements, took a heavy toll and demolition commenced in July 2001. With the exception of its huge chapel and water tower, the only structures left of this once grand institution are the boiler houses and mortuary. It did not have a big reputation for hauntings; however, it was legendary to those fascinated by old abandoned places in the United Kingdom.

Cane Hill. *Courtesy of Chandra Lampreich.*

Central Islip Psychiatric Center

In 1887, New York City purchased 1,000 acres for a farm colony, which resulted in Central Islip. The place officially opened on May 6, 1889, with a total of forty-nine male patients from the city's Wards Island mental facility, but by 1895 the state legislature had put all New York City asylums under Manhattan State Hospital of Central Islip. In 1955, there were 122 buildings, nearly 10,000 patients, and more than 1,000 employees. As with others of its kind, its use steadily declined as therapies improved and the state budget tightened; by 1996, Central Islip Psychiatric Center officially closed. Its remaining patients were transferred to Pilgrim State.

Cliffside Mental Hospital

Like many others of its day preceding the 1930s, Cliffside Mental Hospital was built for the purpose of treating tuberculosis and, like those other facilities, the hospital was later used as a sanitarium to treat psychiatric patients.

According to some local personal accounts, Maude Hutchinson, a young woman in her 20s from Texas, was committed to Cliffside Mental Hospital in the early 1970s. Family and friends began to notice she had become more withdrawn and her anti-social behavior worsened. She would lock herself in her room and continually attempt to create "children" out of household materials, even feeding and clothing them, all the while refusing to eat. This led to her family having her committed. After spending some time in the facility, she became known around the institution simply as "Maude." Many years passed with very little contact with her immediate family, which prompted them to attempt to visit her in the early 1980s, but this was unsuccessful when they learned that she had been transferred in 1979. Despite their best efforts to find her, it soon began to be apparent that this new location was being kept a secret and there has been no reported contact with Maude to the outside world since the 1970s. However, there has been some speculation about the site aunt-maude.blogspot.com, created by a user known as "Maude." It is believed by her family that her drawings are being posted by a worker in the hidden facility. One has to wonder if Maude will ever turn up at this point, as she would be in her sixties by now.

It is believed that not all of the hospital's patient records were moved or destroyed during the transfer. Photos of a group of people touring the facility sometime around 2006, showing multiple boxes of files lining the walls in a special room, are posted online. It is unknown why the hospital did not transfer or destroy these records.

Columbus Psychiatric Hospital

The old State Hospital was truly a massive building that stood on the north side of West Broad Street at the gateway to the Hilltop. The Psychiatric Hospital System in Columbus was established in 1838, but the main building was built between 1870 and 1877. Reports claim it was the biggest building under one roof at the time it was constructed. Dilapidated by the 1980s, the place was falling apart, paint was peeling off the walls, and the cell-like rooms in the basement were eerily vacant, save for an old bed frame. When the final occupants left the place, it stood empty for many years, but then the Ohio Department of Transportation erected a new building on the site — a glass and steel monster as big as the old asylum now stands in its place. The only permanent remnants of the psychiatric complex are the patient cemeteries scattered about the grounds, some visible from Interstate 70.

With a little searching, I located a fascinating article from the *Columbus Dispatch* dated Thursday, October 18, 1894, which during its time had less than high standards of both journalistic and medical ethics. The newspaper published a humorous sidebar about the "Vagaries of the Mind." This interesting article represents a rare glimpse of what plagued the minds of the Columbus Asylum's inmates around the turn of the century.

Vagaries of the Mind

Few Samples from the Columbus Hospital

Big Possessions – "Sea of Death" –
Ex-Policeman With a Hole in His Head, Etc.

The vagaries of the mind are wonderful, even with sane people, but are still more marvelous where reason is dethroned. The old maxim of "many men of many minds" is true, but how insane people can conceive and ride hobbies, such as they do, surpasses human comprehension. One of the inmates of the Columbus Hospital imagines that she owns the institution and issues her orders accordingly. Another is apparently perfectly sane, except when what he calls the "Sea of Death" is brought up. He contends that the sea of death is 18 inches wide, 150 feet deep, and thousands of miles long. No one has ever been able to secure a further explanation than the above.

A former policeman in this city says that he is alright, except his head. When asked for an explanation, he says that there is an opening in the top of his head that is filled with flies. When his head shakes a little, the flies, he says, swarm out and make that buzzing noise that has so often been produced by boys shaking an empty molasses barrel that has been exposed in the summer.

Danvers State Hospital

Danvers Asylum. *Courtesy of Library of Congress.*

In 1878, under the supervision of prominent Boston architect Nathaniel J. Bradlee, the State Lunatic Hospital was erected at the cost of 1.5 million dollars, high atop Hawthorne Hill. Considered to be an architectural masterpiece, Danvers has long been described as a brutally fearsome castle and perverted holy place of despair and destruction. Donned the "witch's castle on the hill," the asylum resides in the town of Danvers, Massachusetts, which many people are unaware was formerly known as Salem Village — the first actual location of the 1692 Salem witch trials. It is believed that some of the condemned were hanged on the hill where Danvers Hospital stands today. So, unlike popular belief, the infamous farce of justice did not begin in Salem, but in Salem Village, or present-day Danvers, at a church on Centre Street. The trials were later moved to a larger building in Salem when hysterical spectators stormed the church.

Interestingly, the most fanatical judge of the witch trials, Jonathan Hawthorne, lived in a house built by his father in 1646 at the top of the hill — the same hill on which the asylum stands today. This is where the name Witch's Castle came from.

The immediate crisis that precipitated the building of a mental hospital north of Boston was the imminence in the early 1870s of the closing of the facility at South Boston. In 1873, Worcester, Taunton, Northampton, and the 1866 Tewksbury Asylum for chronic patients were already housing 1,300 patients in buildings designed for 1,000; another 1,200 were scattered about in various other hospitals. While the hospital was originally established to provide residential treatment and care to the mentally ill, its function expanded to include a training program for nurses in 1889 and a pathological research laboratory in 1895. By the 1920s, the hospital was operating school clinics to help determine mental deficiency in children. During the 1960s, as a result of increased emphasis on alternative methods of treatment and deinstitutionalization and community-based mental health care, the inpatient population started to decrease. Danvers State Hospital closed on June 24, 1992, due to budget cuts within the mental health system. The hospital originally consisted of two main center buildings, housing the administration, with four radiating wings. The administration building measured 90 by 60 feet, with a tower 130 feet high. Connected in the rear was a building 180 by 60 feet, in which the kitchens, laundries, a chapel, and dormitories for the attendants were located. In the rear was a boiler room, over seventy square meters, with boilers that cranked out 450 horsepower used for heating and ventilation. On each side of the main buildings are the wings for male and female patients respectively, connected by small square towers, with the exception of the last ones on each side — they are joined by octagonal towers, measuring ten feet square, used to separate the buildings. The original plan was designed to house five hundred patients, with one hundred more potentially to accommodate in the attic. However, this once humane facility had turned dark by the mid-half of the century.

Danvers, between the decade-long span of 1940 and 1950, housed over 2,600, despite being designed only for a capacity of six hundred. This severe overcrowding caused the staff to turn to unethical medical practices. Customary to infamous asylums of that time, shock treatment, hydrotherapy, and insulin shock therapy were performed, as well as psychosurgeries, such as lobotomies, where the frontal lobe of the brain was removed — this "treatment" was perfected at Danvers. All these barbaric procedures were done to keep its burgeoning population under control. Sadly, this type of solution was a given for its day. "Poorly clothed and sometimes naked, these legions of lost souls were shown pacing aimlessly on the wards, lying on the filthy cement floors, or sitting head in hand against the pock-marked walls," wrote a researcher. Patients became gaunt, dirty, and often spent their days and nights alone, in solitary confinement, in a space no larger than a small cell. It was so bad that a deceased patient would go unnoticed for days. During the 1960s, the alternative methods of treatment, which began a national deinstitutionalization program, led to the patient population starting to decrease and Danvers' eventual closing.

In December 2005, the property was sold to Avalon Bay Development. A lawsuit was filed to stave off the demolition of the hospital, as it is one of the most famous of the Kirkbride buildings and is listed on the National Register of Historic Places. Despite public outcry, demolition of most of the buildings began in January 2006. Mysteriously, on April 7, 2007, four of the new apartment complex buildings and four of the construction trailers burned. The fire was visible from the city of Boston, seventeen miles away. The mysterious fire was confined mostly to the buildings under construction on the eastern end, with damage to the remaining Kirkbride spires. All that remains is the center section of the Kirkbride building, which was the old administration offices, and the wing on each side.

The hospital was the setting for the 1958 film, *Home Before Dark*, and the 2001 horror film, *Session Nine*. I had watched *Session Nine* before I started writing this book and without knowing its connection to the old hospital site. While researching the old building, I was able to recall many of the old rooms that no longer exist. The towers, old residents' rooms, and other places can be seen easily in the movie. The Danvers State Insane Asylum was also the inspiration for H. P. Lovecraft's *Arkham Sanitarium* short stories "Pickman's Model" and "Herbert West Not An Urban Legend," which in turn was the inspiration for the gritty styled painted graphic novel of the Batman comic called *Arkham Asylum* intended for an adult audience. In the book *Project 17* by Laurie Faria Stolarz, the plot centers around six teens breaking into Danvers to investigate the allegedly haunted asylum.

As of this writing, Danvers State is now apartments and, although only part of the original structure was kept, the legend remains alive in the films and fiction that were inspired from it.

Denbigh Asylum (North Wales Hospital)

The North Wales Lunatic Asylum, as it was also called, was the first psychiatric institution built in Wales; construction began in 1844 from plans drawn up by Thomas Fulljames and was completed in 1848 in the town of Denbigh. It is a magnificent example of early Victorian asylum architecture. The U-shaped Tudorbethan style hospital was built after word spread about the mistreatment of Welsh people in English asylums. The North Wales Hospital would be a haven for Welsh-speaking residents to seek treatment without prejudice or a language barrier.

Renovations and extensions were made at the hospital from 1867 to 1956, when the hospital reached its maximum capacity of 1,500 patients and 1,000 staff. Originally Denbigh only housed 200 Welsh patients with mental health problems, but to relieve overcrowding it was later extended, reaching its peak capacity of 1,500 by 1956. Physical treatments, such as Cardiazol, malarial treatment, insulin shock treatment, and sulphur-based drugs, were used and developed in the 1920s and 1930s. The years 1941 and 1942 saw the advent of electro-convulsive therapy (ECT) and prefrontal leucotomy (lobotomy) treatments.

There are 504 confirmed burials of former patients, but there may be as many as 1,000 people buried here; the reason for the uncertainty is because of incomplete or missing state records. Also, the patients' burial markers have sunk below the ground.

Denbigh Asylum. *Courtesy of Mark Davis.*

A book called *Care and Treatment of the Mentally Ill in North Wales, 1800-2000*, by Pamela Michael, describes the rise and fall of the North Wales Hospital from its origins in 1848 to its closure in 1995. The author uses patients' case notes to discuss life in an asylum, to look at changing diagnostic and treatment patterns, and to explore the ways in which ordinary people understood and experienced mental illness. Two movies have been filmed here, *Cider House Rules* and *In Dreams*, both of which came out in 1999. A group of preservation societies lobbied to save the old buildings, to no avail. The developers plan to build a housing community on the site.

On October 31, 2008, *Most Haunted* did a live series, "The Village of the Damned," on location in the North Wales Hospital, which spanned over the course of a week. The producers of the show nicknamed it the "village of the damned" and claimed the place is "cursed by witches." This description, which appears as the official program information on Living TV's *Most Haunted Live*, angered citizens and local paranormal investigators. In fact, padded cells were never used at the North Wales Hospital. Denbigh was finally closed in 1995 because of the appalling conditions of its day and was left to ruin inside from natural decay.

"I am disgusted that this production company have waltzed into Denbigh and seemingly poked fun at mental illness," said Colin Hughes, the former mayor. "This is extremely crass and in bad taste and has upset and insulted a lot of people in the town." The makers of *Most Haunted* told the *Daily Post*: "In no way do we condone the stigmatizing of mental illness or those who suffer with it for the purpose of entertainment. The experiments will in no way belittle or make fun of the patients."

On November 22, 2008, during work to renovate the building site and convert it to apartments and residential properties, the building caught fire and half of the main hall of the hospital was destroyed. Arson was suspected, and huge sections of the floor have rotted through, making navigation difficult, if not life-threatening. Vandals have broken into the institution and stripped it of machinery and destroyed most of the rooms. Possibly due to fear of the dead, the most intact part of Denbigh is its morgue.

Deva Asylum

On the grounds of the Countess of Chester Hospital is the abandoned Deva Asylum. Begun in the year 1829, it was originally designed by William Cole, Jr. to hold up to five hundred patients, but over the years was expanded with new additions to house more than 1,500. The asylum eventually closed in 2005 and since then has lain deserted and completely derelict, though it is surprisingly well preserved. Certain parts are even said to have power and running water while its cramped rooms, discarded patient logs, the labs, and pharmacy are in good condition. One can still gaze in upon the security seclusion cells… An intact dentist's chair is tucked away deep inside the bowels of the service tunnels. Decay is naturally present in the old tiled corridors and stone spiral steps, but the old treatment center has a feel of unease unmatched in a way from others. Its ghostliness has an eerie untouched quality…as if deserted in silent mystery.

Dixmont State Hospital

The Dixmont State Hospital, originally the Department of the Insane in the Western Pennsylvania Hospital of Pittsburg, was a hospital located northwest of the city. Managers of the hospital used a $10,000 appropriation from the state to purchase a large amount of farmland on a hill overlooking the Ohio River, to the north of Pittsburgh. The institution first opened with a grand ceremony on July 19, 1859. When the cornerstone of the Dixmont Kirkbride building was laid in the foundation, workers set a glass jar in the cornerstone; this jar contained numerous objects, papers, and a letter from Dorothea Dix, as well as a copy of her *1845 Memorial*, the 55-page county by county study of the conditions for the mentally ill in Pennsylvania. It was, as I mentioned in the Introduction, one of the key works that fostered a major change in how facilities were run. The original patient population of the hospital was 113, most of whom were transfers from the Western Pennsylvania Hospital in Pittsburgh. In 1907, the facility was individually incorporated as the Dixmont Hospital for the Insane after separating from the Western Pennsylvania Hospital system. It had 1,500 patients in its care.

The Hutchinson Building was where the infirmary was located. It also had isolation units, a laboratory, morgue, and rooms where electroshock therapy, lobotomies, and autopsies were performed. Each floor had patient rooms on the ends of the building, built in a circular pattern around the glass-walled nurses' station. The geriatric center of Dixmont was built in the early 1950s. Now renovated and renamed the Verland Foundation for the Disabled, the property is owned by the family that purchased it.

The facility saw its demise in 1984. A fire had completely gutted the administration building, which was already in a sad state of deterioration, so in 1999 the state sold the 407-acre property. In 2005, an agreement was in place to demolish it for a Walmart Supercenter. Subsequent excavation destabilized the hillside and landslides toppled over the highway and railroad tracks, causing them to close for nearly a month. On September 26, 2007, after complaints poured in from local residents who feared another collapse amid concern about the land's instability, Walmart decided not to build on the property and allowed the land to revert back to its natural condition. Regardless of their choice, they would have been prevented in the conversion, as Pennsylvania law prohibits the sale of gravesites. Locals avoid the area out of a curious wonder that the landslides were *not* naturally caused.

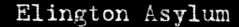

Elington Asylum

Although I attempted to contain the majority of the asylums to the United States, a few in other countries stood out that just had to be included. One of these was visited by a friend of mine and he felt it was "one of the creepiest, in one of the creepiest cities," in Europe. Located on the Lee River in Ireland, it is also one of the largest and one of the oldest sanitariums there is. I made note of this particular asylum due to the fact people who live there have made mention that many places in the city of Cork are haunted, including a two-story house that a priest stopped living in due to creepy feelings he experienced (he later found out that someone had hanged themselves there!); the old jail (gaol in the old way of saying it); St. Kevin's Hospital, also in the Sunday's Well area; and, of course, the Atkins Hall Apartments, which used to be the insane asylum known as Elington, or Cork Asylum. I spoke to photographer, Mark Davis, who explored this old sanitarium, and he was gracious enough to pass along the local history.

Author's Note: The following is copied by permission from Mark Davis, who also generously took the pictures accompanying it.

Our Lady's Hospital, formerly Elington Asylum, Cork, was built to house 500 patients. It was the largest of seven district lunatic asylums commissioned by the Board of Public Works in the late 1840s to supplement the nine establishments erected by Johnston and Murray in 1820-35. Like the earlier buildings, the new institutions were 'corridor asylums,' but with the emphasis on wards rather than cells. There was a change in style from Classical to Gothic. Designed by local architect William Atkins, the Cork Asylum was one of the longest buildings in Ireland (almost 1,000 feet), originally split into three blocks punctuated with towers and gables. Atkins made good use of polychromy, contrasting Glanmire sandstone with limestone dressings. The elevated site, overlooking the River Lee at Shanakiel, appears to have been chosen by the local Governors for dramatic effect rather than practicality, great difficulty being encountered in providing exercise yards on the steep slope. The Asylum had three stories. Construction cost including site £79,827..1/5d A Distressing Account from 1988, Debated in the Irish Parliament, on the Decline of the Hospital. The issue I have raised is the report of the Inspector of Mental Hospitals on conditions in Our Lady's Hospital in Cork. I propose to devote a considerable period of my time to extracts from the report of the Inspector of Mental Hospitals because, even though it is a very late hour and even though I, like everybody else, would like to go home, there are things in that report that need to be put on the record of this House and on the record of the Houses of the Oireachtas. The first thing that needs to be said is that there are about 1,000 patients in Our Lady's Hospital in Cork and almost all of them, with the exception of about thirty or forty, are long-stay patients. The Inspector of Mental Hospitals visited that hospital in February of this year. I want to put on the record of this House brief extracts about a variety of wards.

St. Kevin's 5, a female ward with twenty-eight patients: There was one toilet off the dormitory and five toilets off the dayroom, which were dirty.

St. Kevin's 6, a male ward with eighteen patients: Some renovation work was going on in this ward. The dormitory was locked off during the day. Each patient had a wardrobe. There was no soap and no towels were available. The toilet area off the dormitory was dirty and there were no curtains on the windows. We are not talking about prisons or shelters for the homeless; we are talking about a hospital.

St. Kevin's 8, female, with twenty-one patients: A washing machine to wash the clothes of the patients was bought from patients' money. The toilet had no seat and there were no curtains. The whole report could well be read onto the record, a Chathaoirligh, but I do not propose to do that.

St. Patrick's 1, male, with twenty-two patients: All windows in the toilet were broken and had been covered by sheets of plywood; it was dirty. One dormitory had thirteen beds and no curtains. One patient had gone to bed. Another dormitory had eight beds with no curtains. There was no ward programme and the whole ward lacked any visual stimulation.

St. Ita's 1, female, with twenty patients: The enclosed courtyard attached to the ward was littered with old clothing, toilet rolls, and plastic bottles, which had accumulated over several months. We were informed that patients do not get out of doors in winter time. The dormitory with seven beds had no curtains. Many patients were in bed for the night at the time of our visit — 5.15 p.m. Another dormitory housed ten patients and was also without curtains. Five beds were placed along one wall while on the opposite wall a structure had been erected in which five patients were separately incarcerated. Each unit was roofed in the manner of a stall and each door was closed by three farmyard bolts. Mattresses were generally on the floor. These units did not have external windows or fresh air. There was a padded cell with a mattress on the floor of this ward. Toilets had no seats and there was no soap available to patients.

On this particular part, the inspector had the following to say: "Regrettably the dining arrangements on the wards were equally bad. Hot food is taken to the wards in containers, which are neither heated nor insulated. On the ward, we saw patients' lunches being divided into portions and placed in a heated trolley, which was not hot enough to keep them warm. Potatoes of poor quality had been placed on the table even though patients had not by then begun to take their places. Almost inevitably patients would be eating cold lunches. No effort is made to make eating an enjoyable experience."

The first recommendation made on that part is to restore the beds that were taken down in St. Anne's Hospital as a consequence of the cutbacks. There is a lot more.

On the North Cork area, Ita's 5, female, eighteen beds, the reports says: Like many other wards the windows were dirty and many panes of glass were cracked or broken. The window nearest the entrance on the corridor had twenty-three broken or cracked panes of glass. *Ita's 6, female, eighteen beds* — two toilets off the dormitory had no seats. The windows were dirty. *St. Patrick's, 5, thirteen patients* — the walls in the dayroom were peeled and blistered. There were no pictures on the walls. The toilet area was fairly poor. One of the two toilets had a seat. There were twelve broken panes of glass in the bathroom [1936] window. There was no patients' centre for work. *St. Patrick's, 11, twenty-two beds* — the toilets were generally dirty, but they had seats.

General comments on wards in this area: Milk comes to wards in, we were told, open buckets. This is because the milk is purchased in bulk thereby effecting a saving of about £3,000 than if it were to be bought in cartons. In some wards, there is no adequate facility for storing food. In one ward, we saw bread being stored in dust bins, most of it stale. Laundry facilities are not satisfactory in that units experience difficulty in getting their own clothes or bed linen back. We are told that most of the laundry staff was taking voluntary redundancy, that the machinery is antiquated and frequently breaks down and is in urgent need of overhauling. This would cost £200,000.

This report goes on and on and on: "St. Kevin's, 9, male, twenty-eight patients — there is no activity in the dayroom. The patients sat around in armchairs waiting for bed time, which was somewhere between 5.30 p.m. and 6.30 p.m. The washhand basin area was used to store all sorts of rubbish. One window had four broken panes of glass. Again, in that area it is recommended that the fifteen beds taken from the acute unit by the cutbacks be restored.

West Cork is covered with less detail. *Patrick's 8, twenty-nine male patients* — there are no curtains on the dormitory or on the corridor. General comment on the ward in this area: there is evidence of lack of activity and occupation for patients although some patients do leave the ward to go to occupational therapy. Again, in that area there is a recommendation for restoration of the cutbacks.

Having catalogued this "chapter of horrors," as the Cork Examiner described it, the inspector went on to make some general comments about Our Lady's. I want to put these on the record of the House. "The exterior of Our Lady's Hospital can only be described as filthy. Rubbish, litter, discarded toilet rolls are to be seen in profusion around the bases of the building, behind the grey building, behind St. Kevin's and in internal courtyards. Connecting corridors and walkways, particularly within the old building and leading therefrom to, for example, the industrial therapy centre, are dirty beyond description. Saucers of milk" — and I am talking now about a psychiatric hospital — "and other food are left out for cats. However, those cats must fulfill some function as many of the wards are mice-infested. One of our party saw some mice during the inspection and there may even be rats around." This is a hospital we are talking about. "We did see one carcass. Internally, some but not all wards are dirty with windows grimed with opaque matter and walls peeling. These latter states of affairs were particularly evident in the main mentally handicapped ward in the grey building, St. Patrick's 1. Generally wards, particularly male wards, lacked curtains. There was a general feeling of crowdedness and a great single open space in some of the dormitories and in none of them was there any satisfactory attempt at dividing sleeping areas into warm, homely comfortable subdivisions. Lavatories, too, were generally unsatisfactory with lavatory seats missing and in some cases floors dirty and wet.

"Earlier redundancies among nursing staffs were to have coincided with significant ward closures. The redundancies happened, but the ward closures did not. The result is that the remaining staff is spread thinly over too many wards. It is not possible to establish cogent reasons why the ward closures did not go ahead as planned."

General comments on Cork psychiatric services: This is the comment of the Inspector of Mental Hospitals — "Our impression of the approach to the delivery of mental health care in Cork city and county is that it is seriously deficient from a planning point of view. No clear objectives appear to have been identified, no priorities delineated and their solutions adopted. There appears to be a lack of clear lines of command and proper structured consultation. In addition, there seems to be industrial unrest, which has never been adequately dealt with. This has hindered progress in providing adequate services and bringing about change. This is most notably evident in the illegal opposition to the transfer of patients from Our Lady's to Sarsfield Court. This was a disgraceful episode, which reflects no credit on anybody and exemplifies management's inability or unwillingness to direct the service in the interests of the patients."

I want to emphasise that. The Inspector of Mental Hospitals clearly identified the responsibility in this matter as a responsibility of management. It reflects management's inability or unwillingness to direct the service in the interests of patients.

The report continues: "Equally disturbing is the manner in which management has taken, apparently without consultation, decisions to curtail the vital community and acute aspects of the service." I did not say that the management had cut back on the services, the Inspector of Mental Hospitals Services did. "The withdrawal of community nurses, the suppression of beds in the Regional Hospital unit in St. Anne's while leaving intact the entire ladies' complex is incomprehensible and can only lead to the transfer of more patients to Our Lady's. Our Lady's costs approximately £10 million to £11 million annually to run. The service provided by the hospital is extremely poor and for the most part appears to provide the worst form of custodial care. The majority of patients are unoccupied and no attempt is made to provide appropriate rehabilitative inputs for them on their wards. It is our view that the board should establish and operate proper management techniques in relation to the whole Cork service. This should involve as primary objectives the prevention of further admissions to Our Lady's, which cannot provide up-to-date psychiatric care of a standard commensurate with proper human dignity and an intensive rehabilitation programme for existing in-patients."

That is the view of the Inspector of Mental Hospitals, together with those who assisted him on that inspection. I have frequently talked in this House [1939] about the conditions of the homeless and of travellers and of prisoners. I know that you, a Chathaoirligh, have a considerable concern about the welfare of the mentally handicapped. The institution whose appalling record I have just read onto the record of this House does house, if that is the right word — I would say probably "contain" is a better description — many mentally handicapped people. I have talked about this matter in this House. I have never — and at 3 o'clock in the morning it is not possible to start acting about things — in my life been so outraged about something. To be truthful I have, perhaps, been more outraged about one thing and that was the condition of some children I saw once. With that exception I have never been so outraged as I have been by this report. I have known, and most of Cork has known or suspected, that the hospital was a disgrace. That was the position until we got this independent, authoritative written document — and incidentally, I did not say it at the beginning, the fact that I have it in my possession renders me in breach of the Official Secrets Act because it is not a public document, but I have it and I am very glad to have it. It is among the most appalling, distressing, disturbing, offensive documents I have ever had the misfortune to read. The people in Our Lady's Hospital are guilty of nothing. They are vulnerable, innocent, and, in the old Irish phrase, in the area of the country that the Minister comes from and that I have close connections with, they would be described as "harmless." They do not deserve what is being done to them. They are victims of misfortune; they are victims of illness and indeed, tragically, of abandonment. They deserve our best. They have got our worst. Instead we lock them up in a vermin-infested — not my conclusion, but the inspector's conclusion — unsanitary — not my conclusion but the inspector's conclusion — dirty, dark confinement. It is a disgrace. When you consider that we make them all, old age pensioners, pay for it. We take most of [1940] their income, the best part of £40 a week from them. They pay for that confinement, that locking up in dirty unsanitary conditions. We have to and must make very fundamental choices. It is a disgrace that people have been paid large salaries, salaries twice and three times the average industrial wage, to manage such an institution of confinement. Those people have failed to discharge their duties. They should resign or be sacked. Messrs. Denis Dudley, Donal O'Sullivan, and Pettit should either resign or be sacked. They are unfit for their job. They are a disgrace to their profession and they should be dispensed with.

An Leas-Chathaoirleach: In fairness, would the Senator withdraw those remarks? You cannot name people if they are not here to defend themselves.

Mr. B. Ryan: I have named them and I make no apology for naming them. They are not accountable to anybody I know for what they do. Tell me where I can make them accountable?

An Leas-Chathaoirleach: I am not making an excuse for the hour of the morning, but it is abusing the privilege of the House to name people when they cannot protect themselves. There is a long-standing rule of the House that this is never done.

Mr. B. Ryan: Many people have been named in this House—

An Cathaoirleach: But not in the form that you have just named them, which is in a critical fashion. We are not going to have a dispute at this time.

Mr. B. Ryan: I do not wish to withdraw the names. I am sorry. I do not propose to pursue it any further.

An Cathaoirleach: Let us conclude.

Mr. B. Ryan: Once we clear out the system, we should forget about cosmetics and do the only thing possible, that is, close down the place once and for all.

An Cathaoirleach: Senator Ryan, I am afraid you named three people who are not here to defend themselves. If you will not withdraw their names, we will have to conclude.

Mr. B. Ryan: The victims of their neglect are not here either and nobody will defend them. (Interruptions.)

Michael O'Kennedy, Minister for Agriculture and Food (Mr. O'Kennedy): I regret that my colleague, the Minister for Health, who has a very deep concern about issues of this nature is not here at this hour of the morning to respond to the matter on the Adjournment due to the manner in which the business of the House has been conducted during the course of a long night and early morning. I hope that the Members of the House and all the staff involved will appreciate that it is no indication of lack of interest on his part that he is not here. For my own part, I have been here for almost twelve hours now and, before addressing the House on behalf of my colleague, the Minister for Health, may I express my appreciation to you, a Chathaoirligh, your staff, and the press for their attendance during what has been a protracted debate to no particular purpose. The business which brought me here is a very serious business, and I regret to have to say at this point that it was used and abused by some Members of the House for a purpose that was not meant to be in the interest of the legislation we were discussing. I would have wished to have had the opportunity of replying, but circumstances, which I accept as the procedure of the House, did not enable me to do that. I have the privilege to reply now at this hour on behalf of my colleague. I want to indicate to the House that this is the reply of my colleague, who has given a lot of thought and attention to this issue raised by Senator Ryan. I quote precisely from what my colleague, the Minister for Health, Deputy Dr. O'Hanlon, would have said: "As the Senator is no doubt aware, the management and operation of Our Lady's

Hospital, Cork, is the concern of the Southern Health Board. Under the provisions of the Mental Treatment Act, 1945, the Inspector of Mental Hospitals is obliged to make a formal inspection of each district mental hospital every year and to submit a report to me on his inspection. Earlier this year the inspector visited Our Lady's Hospital and subsequently submitted a report to me. That report was critical of both the hospital and the psychiatric services in the area. I sent copies of the report to the chief executive officer of the board for his views. I understand copies of the relevant sections of the report were sent to the clinical directors concerned and that copies of the report were sent to the members of the psychiatric services committee of the board. I have been considering the inspector's comments and his recommendations as to how the shortcoming he reported could be overcome. I have had detailed discussions with senior officers of my Department, including the Inspector of Mental Hospitals, prior to having discussions with the chairman and the chief executive officer of the health board, which will take place very shortly. These discussions will have two objectives. First will be the steps which need to be taken as a matter of urgency to improve the very unsatisfactory conditions described by the inspector. I would include in that the creation of structures which will ensure not only that improvements are made but also that they are maintained. It is disappointing to find the report critical of the physical conditions in an institution on which my Department spent almost £1 million in recent years under the minor capital scheme, in addition to the board's own maintenance. The second objective will be to bring about organizational changes in the psychiatric service in Cork city and county. The ultimate solution to the problems which exist in Our Lady's Hospital will only be found in the development of a psychiatric service based in the community. In line with national policy, I feel it is essential to decentralize the current psychiatric services in Cork and develop a network of community based facilities. This is in keeping with the policy outlined in Planning for the Future. Our Lady's Hospital services four catchment areas, each of which should have its own admission and acute care unit, day hospitals, out-patient clinics, day centres, hostels, and other small scale facilities. In this way admissions to Our Lady's Hospital would cease. Instead patients could be treated at or near their homes. Only a small proportion require in-patient care and usually for a short time only. A psychiatric service based on this model would be of great benefit to patients and would prevent the build up of long stay patients such as we have at present in our psychiatric hospitals. Part of the reorganization of the service will be the rehabilitation of existing long stay patients. A significant proportion of the 900 patients now in Our Lady's Hospital could and should be enabled to leave the hospital and live in ordinary houses in the community. In my discussions with the chairman and chief executive officer, I expect it will become clear what steps are necessary now to bring about the desired changes. I will be anxious to help in bringing them about."

An Cathaoirleach: Before we adjourn, I would like to put on the record that I deeply regret that Senator Ryan did not withdraw his charge against the three named individuals. In fairness, Senator Ryan abused the privilege of this House and I would like to put it on record that I would not like him to do that again. As it is now 3.15 a.m., the House stands adjourned until 10.30 this morning.

Cork's longest building in the country — the former Eglinton Lunatic Asylum — was built with long, long corridors so the loonies would never have to go around the bend. The main structure has been partly converted to flats and renamed Atkins Hall after the architect.

Essex Mountain Sanitarium

On what is now the site of Verona High School used to be the spot for a home for wayward girls in 1900. However, after a fire destroyed the building, the Essex Mountain Sanatorium was opened in its place in 1907. For nearly seventy years, it ran with almost complete anonymity. It wasn't until investigations began involving allegations of patient mistreatment that the school suddenly closed its doors in 1977, with hundreds of patient files everywhere and facilities left untouched. Much like the abandoned Deva Asylum, it was almost as if everyone had simply disappeared...

By the early 1980s, other stories of the former sanitarium being haunted began to circulate, as well as reports that a Devil worship took place in the chapel. Occult graffiti was visible throughout the complex. Reported paranormal activity was claimed by visitors: sounds of distant footsteps and disembodied voices, as well as ghostly apparitions of the former violent patients who returned to haunt both the buildings and underground tunnel system.

Another account came in from an explorer of the ruins: As they looked towards the big building, they noticed that about four or five floors up, there was someone looking down at them from one of the windows. If fact, it would lend credence to the claims of past visitors about pictures of faces that were taken in the infirmary in 1918. Further eye-witness accounts from explorers say that exit signs were still lit above the stairway doors and body parts were still in a room on the top floor of the main building, sitting there on a shelf in formaldehyde, such as a brain, a heart, and a tapeworm, that was removed from a forty-year-old woman, according to the description on the side of the jar.

The sanitarium has since been demolished.

Essex County Isolation Hospital in Belleville, New Jersey.
Courtesy Chandra Lampreich.

Foxboro State Hospital

Foxboro State Hospital, located in Massachusetts, opened in 1889 as a place that was known for treating alcoholism as a disease, but eventually it transformed into an institution for the mentally ill. It closed in 1976, but former visitors were reported to have heard and witnessed "doors closing, sounds that come from nowhere, shadows moving, and other strange things happen all the time."

One person claimed that their father worked at Foxboro until its closing and that he mentioned "…many interesting things happened there at night when everyone was asleep. Things turning themselves on for example… There is a bowling alley in the basement and the pins were manually set. There were no machines. I remember one day being one of the only people in the building and hearing bowling balls and going down there and seeing the pins set-up that were not before. The buildings still remain, and strange things do happen. For instance you could hear and see the outside doors trying to be pushed out, as if they were trying to escape. Others believe these are the spirits that have been beaten severely or have been tortured. Reported by a former employee at the hospital during the 1980s that Buildings A and B were freezing no matter what the weather was. Doors slam shut, and the feeling of being watched."

Others say they see eerie figures walking around the construction site of the buildings that have been converted. Other buildings are still empty. A lonely chimney marks the center of the property. The location has two cemeteries located within a mile of the main complex. The Foxboro Jaycees had a haunted house on the location every Halloween for almost twenty years, but were asked to stop in early 2008. The site has since been demolished.

These images are from Saint Augustine asylum, they are indicative of the "surgery centers" most sanitariums of that day had.
Courtesy of Dawid Jagusiak.

Gaebler Children's Center

An episode of *Scariest Places on Earth* showcased a sanitarium/mental asylum in New England, rumored to be the Metropolitan State Hospital for the mentally ill, located in Waltham, Massachusetts. Closed in January 1992 as a result of state budget cuts, the Gaebler Children's Center for mentally ill youths, located on the grounds of the hospital, has become a popular destination for urban explorers, despite both security and physical safety concerns. Since 2005, the large complex of buildings has been gradually undergoing demolition. Vacant since the center's closing in 1992, there is not much left to look at, as it would seem vandals and ghost hunters had already visited the Trapelo Road building. Windows were broken, furniture was gone, and many doors had been taken off the hinges and scrapped for copper. The back entrance was even unlocked.

Patient Murder Scandal: In 1978, Metropolitan State patient Anne Marie Davee was murdered by another patient, Melvin W. Wilson, who dismembered Davee's body yet kept seven of her teeth; these were discovered in his possession by employees of the hospital. Despite this discovery and its obvious implications, no action was taken against Wilson until Massachusetts State Senator Jack Backman (D-Brookline) led a Senate investigation into the case, along with nineteen other reports of negligence by state mental health workers.

On August 12, 1980, Wilson led investigators to at least three burial sites where he put pieces of Davee's body. Much of the material evidence in the case had been destroyed or gone missing. This evidence included a hut in the woods, where Davee and Wilson had met, clothes, and even sheets, which hospital employees discovered the day after her disappearance. Nearly two months after her murder, another search by hospital staff yielded pieces of Davee's clothing and belongings — and a hatchet, the supposed murder weapon. See also *All of God's Little Angel's*, a documentary. In the early 1960s, Met State had an active children's ward. Before the Davee/Wilson case, more than two dozen preteens died and were buried on the grounds. It is rumored that the preteens were poisoned with strontium that had been put in their milk by doctors who believed it would effectively treat them. It is generally thought to be haunted by local children and teenagers.

Katherine Anderson's self-published book, *Behind the Walls: Shadows of New England's Asylums*, features photographs from nineteen abandoned New England psychiatric hospital buildings, including Gaebler, Metropolitan State Hospital, Belmon's McLean Hospital, and the Walter E. Fernald School. The author said Gaebler was one of the most frightening places she's ever been, reporting: "They used large skeleton keys to lock them, almost like you'd see on the door of a prison." Inside, she saw many of the isolation rooms with metal doors, huge key locks, and small rectangular windows.

As referenced in her book, Anderson interviewed former Gaebler resident Andrew Palmer, who described the hospital to be like a prison and referred to the staff as "the human zoo keepers." Palmer was once considered one of the least functioning children at the institution, Anderson said, but he grew up to become an advocate for the rights of mental health patients. Anderson also spoke with a former mental health assistant from Waltham's Metropolitan State Hospital, which was closed in 1992. Michael Stowe worked at the hospital in the late 1980s when the pay was $3 an hour and all he could afford was a "roach-infested" apartment nearby.

On his blog www.goodjobsucking.com, Stow recounts stories about getting lost in the hospital's underground tunnels and trying to discourage his Haitian co-workers from speaking French to keep them from being attacked by paranoid patients.

Waltham Mayor Jeannette McCarthy said police increased patrols in the area after discovering that the buildings were showing up in YouTube videos. In one such video, posted in November 2006, someone is walking through the hospital corridors with a dim flashlight to illuminate doors and discarded objects. All you can hear is heavy breathing and footsteps. Another video is a collection of photographs from the children's psychiatric facility: the rusted playground, a piano with a roll of toilet paper, and a roller skate that someone left behind.

McCarthy said if a photographer wants to go inside one of the vacant buildings a permit is required. The city received a few such requests from filmmakers over the years, but McCarthy discouraged use of the old Trapelo Road site because the buildings are contaminated with asbestos. This is why the city, which now owns the property, plans to demolish Gaebler and the site for recreation, McCarthy said. Demolition officially occurred between November 2010 and January 2011.

Genesee County (Rolling Hills Asylum)

Located somewhere between Buffalo and Rochester, sits an enormous brick building on a hill in East Bethany, New York. Opened on January 1, 1827, Rolling Hills Asylum was originally known as the Genesee County Poor Farm and was created by the county to house those eligible for assistance — which meant the poor, the town drunks, and the lunatics, mixed in with the undesirables, such as the blind, the handicapped, orphans, and widows. In the 1990s, the building was renovated into a set of shops and an antiques mall. When the property's vendors and shoppers began to notice strange occurrences, a paranormal group was called in to investigate the building. After that, Rolling Hills' reputation grew and it soon became a popular spot for ghost hunters who report voices, doors frozen shut, screams at night, and what is known as shadow people.

Rolling Hills Case Manager, Suzie Yencer, relates her frightening experience: "It was September 2007. While working a public hunt, we had a gentleman with us that was filming a documentary about the building. He wanted to try an experiment in one of the rooms. The room he chose was in the basement, popularly known as The Christmas Room. The experiment he wanted to try was to sit in the room with no lights or equipment on. The only light we would use was a pink glow stick in the middle of a circle of people. We also placed a small ball and a toddler size rocking horse in the circle. The gentleman conducting the experiment requested that only I talk and try to make contact with the spirits. The more I talked, the more strange occurrences began to happen. The glow stick started to move back and forth, and the rocking horse began to slowly rock. A few of the guests in the room including myself saw a hand and arm come out of nowhere and reach for the ball in the circle and then just vanish...."

From the website on the place itself, the owners wish to express their feelings by saying they "...are thrilled by all the interest in Rolling Hills Asylum and LOVE meeting the people who come to investigate or even just out of curiosity. However, please keep in mind this is private property and is owner occupied! So please, be respectful and refrain from wandering about the property at whim. If you are driving by, feel free to take pictures from the front steps of the infirmary, but please do not stroll about the property like it is a public park. Our dogs wander the property freely and you risk getting bit or worse. Please understand this is private property and my family LIVES here. The dogs are secured during hunts and tours, but the rest of the time they are free to enjoy their HOME. RHA is not public property — it is private property and privately owned by Sharon. We open it up to the public on select dates for people to enjoy and learn about the history and the spirits here. All we are asking for is a little respect. After all, we'd never pull up to your house, get out of the car, and begin strolling around your property, backyard, barns, or garages. It just isn't appropriate and it's trespassing."

Genesee County Poor Farm, Rolling Hills Asylum.
Courtesy of Tim Shaw.

Glenn Dale Hospital Mission

Glenn Dale opened in the same era as Fairfield State — the 1930s — as a tuberculosis hospital, with one building for adults and one for children. Eventually the tuberculosis problem died down and Glenn Dale was repurposed. It closed in 1982 due to asbestos and structural problems, but before it closed it was (supposedly) home to the criminally insane. As with Fairfield State, the buildings are connected via underground passageways, which people have been exploring since the day Glenn Dale officially closed its doors.

One rumor says that when the hospital closed, the remaining patients were just turned loose. Having nowhere else to go, many of them simply broke back into the abandoned buildings and lurk there even today.

Another story goes that a police officer went to check out the buildings himself after getting a call that they were being vandalized by a group of kids. After he went in, someone in the vicinity heard gunshots and called the police. When the police arrived, they found the first officer standing in one of the rooms, staring straight ahead at nothing. He had emptied his gun firing at something that no one ever found.

Great Barr Colony (St. Margaret's Hospital)

A huge mansion known as the Great Barr Hall had its beginnings in the seventeenth century, but was extensively remodeled throughout the nineteenth century.

The Lunar Society, an informal group of leading engineers, industrialists, scientists, and thinkers of the day, met here in the early 1800s. The estate is built on the grounds of the old St. Margaret's mental hospital in Great Barr — or the "Great Barr Idiot Colony," as it was originally called in the less enlightened early 1900s.

The estate sits on a substantially sized lake, part of Great Barr park, which the Hall used to overlook. The lake is completely fenced off, stopping residents or anybody else from enjoying its beauty. Surrounding the lake, and indeed the estate, is the woods.

Great Barr Hall was originally built in 1777 by Joseph Scott. In 1791, it was inherited by Sir Francis Scott, who lived there until his death in 1863; Sir Francis' widow, Mildred, remained at the Hall until her death in 1909. It was much altered and extended about 1840 and, in 1863, an adjacent chapel (which was never consecrated and was used as a billiard room) was erected.

In 1911, the Hall and its grounds were purchased by the Walsall and West Bromwich Joint Board, a hospital board that used it "for the reception of poor persons requiring relief on account of bodily or mental infirmity" after the First World War. It became known as the Great Barr Park Idiot Colony, and there had been reports made by nursing staff at the hospital that the ghost of Sir Joseph Scott had been seen amongst the ruins of his once home. Also, the ghost of a grey lady used to be seen in mid-air (floating) walking down the area where the great staircase once stood. The colony was later renamed St. Margaret's Hospital.

Great Barr Hall, a Gothic mansion, has stood in some form or another since the late 1700s. It was used as part of the hospital between 1918 until the hospital's closing in 1978, and then left to decay. The main buildings of St. Maggie's, as locals call it, are completely gone; however, what was known as Great Barr Hall still stands, albeit in a state of disrepair, having been partially burnt to the ground. In 2006, the estate was brought by a developer and more than four hundred houses were built on the site.

Greystone Park Psychiatric Hospital

Greystone Park Psychiatric Hospital.
Courtesy of Nan Guzauski.

A view of the chapel at Greystone Park Psychiatric Hospital. *Courtesy of Nan Guzauski.*

The New Jersey State Hospital, opened in August 1876, was originally called the New Jersey State Lunatic Asylum or Morris Plains State Hospital. It was built in the Kirkbride design and did not get its current name until 1924. The hospital was built to relieve overcrowding in what was then the state's only asylum in Trenton. It was also built as a central location to the more populated northern half of the state. However, the new hospital quickly became overcrowded, housing its eight hundred patients in a facility designed for only the initial six hundred beds.

Beauty shop, Greystone Park Psychiatric Hospital. *Courtesy of Nan Guzauski.*

The Currie Building, Greystone Park Psychiatric Hospital. *Courtesy of Nan Guzauski.*

The medical building at Greystone Park Psychiatric Hospital. *Courtesy of Nan Guzauski.*

To alleviate the overcrowding, separate dormitories were built, but they also became so overcrowded that the dining rooms had to be converted to rooms. By 1914, the facility had a staggering population of 2,412 patients. By the end of the Second World War, the population had reached its peak of 7,674 patients in the early 1950s. The site officially closed in 2000 and had been largely abandoned.

The hospital was closed for many reasons, not the least of which was lack of funding, but largely due to some serious problems and allegations, including patient suicide, patient pregnancy, a sexual assault in an elevator, and the escape of a convicted rapist. At that time, the site covered over a square mile and consisted of forty-three buildings. In 2005, many of the outlying buildings were torn down and a park was created by the county. In 2007, a new mental health hospital opened behind the old main building. In 2008, further buildings were demolished, including the Curry Building, when they were deemed unsafe and unsalvageable. Today the remaining standing structures (including the main building) are for sale while being currently owned by the state.

The Greystone is where the television show *House* was filmed at the end of Season 5 and the beginning of Season 6. It was also used for *Paranormal Activity*, which attempted to show the ghost of Woody Guthrie; the legendary singer-songwriter has been said to haunt the site, wandering aimlessly in a daze. After a night in jail, Guthrie was sent to Greystone Park State Hospital, where he was eventually diagnosed with Huntington's disease, an incurable illness characterized by involuntary movements and a deterioration of mental faculties. He was committed here in 1956 and died from Huntington's disease in 1967. With some humor, Guthrie referred to the hospital as "Gravestone" and the ward he stayed on as "Wardy Forty."

Another incident was a patient being shot to death by security while trying to escape through the tunnels under the hospital. Other typically reported activity from such locations, including echoing footsteps, distant screams, apparitions of former patients and staff, light anomalies, and doors and windows opening and closing on their own, are said to occur here.

Haverford State Hospital

Haverford State Hospital was an abandoned mental institution on the northern outskirts of Delaware County, west of the city of Philadelphia, in Haverford Township. Originally constructed in 1964 as a state-of-the-art hospital, its patients enjoyed private rooms and recreational activities, such as bowling. The entire complex consisted of seventeen buildings, the largest being the Acute Intensive Care Center named Hilltop, and had an enormous boiler plant, garage, head administration building, recreation building, five treatment wards, and two geriatric wards. Its closure in 1998 was due in part to a lawsuit using the Americans with Disabilities Act as well as the general deinstitutionalization of the state hospital system. When it closed, most of the patients were transferred to Norristown State Hospital.

On November 14, 2006, the Haverford Township Board of Commissioners approved the Agreement of Sale and Preliminary Land Development Plans, which will build several hundred condominiums. The township plans to build several athletic fields. Demolition of the former state hospital began in early June 2007; the first buildings taken down were the administration and recreation buildings, followed by the extended treatment and geriatric wards.

Hellingly Asylum

Sitting atop a hill overlooking east Hailsham, in East Sussex, in England's countryside, stands the forlorn remains of Hellingly Asylum, which first opened its doors to patients in 1903 and continued to serve the local community for nearly one hundred years. The hospital, also known as East Sussex County Asylum or, just simply, Hellingly, was the concept of architect G. T. Hine, one of the great asylum architects of his day, and built in a late Victorian design during a period of massive expansion for mental health facilities in England. The hospital had its own railway line, the Hellingly Hospital Railway, used principally for transport of coal; the rail led from the main line to the boiler house. The hospital also had a vast laundry room, ball room, patients' shop, sewing rooms, and nurses' home as well.

The majority of the hospital closed in 1994, but to this day much of the vast site stands nearly demolished after suffering repeated vandalism. Arson has also destroyed several buildings, most notably the administration block. Trespassers have broken all the windows and the interior has suffered just as much. Its winding halls are filled with mounds of rubble from collapsing floors. The hospital was made popular with the television show, *Urban Explorers*.

Hellingly Asylum.
Courtesy of Dawid Jagusaik.

High Royds Asylum

With its 130-foot-tall clock tower dominating the surrounding West Yorkshire landscape, High Royds Asylum boasts aging yet beautiful Italian mosaics and detailed tile work. Standing on nearly three hundred acres, it is currently being redeveloped for housing. It is in shockingly good condition, which is quite possibly why it is not being torn down but rather reworked.

Opened in 1888 as the West Riding Pauper Lunatic Asylum, High Royds was designed by J. Vickers-Edwards and is arguably the finest example of a broad arrow layout. Self-contained like Hellingly and West Park, High Royds formerly boasted a library, surgery rooms, butchers, dairy, tailor, sweet shop, bakers, and cobblers, as well as its own railway. At its peak, High Royds could care for more than 1,000 patients. During World War Two, it treated soldiers injured in battle.

The Local Government Act of 1888 brought about a major change in the government of the county asylums. High Royds was one of the last remaining psychiatric hospitals still functioning when it closed in 2003.

High Royds Asylums. *Courtesy of Mark Davis.*

A view of a padded cell at High Royds Asylum.
Courtesy of Mark Davis.

The Hudson River State Hospital

The Hudson River State Hospital is a former New York state psychiatric hospital whose main building had been designated a National Historic Landmark. It is also one of the best looking examples of High Victorian Gothic architecture, the first use of that style for an American institutional building.

The main building, like so many others that followed the Kirkbride example, separated the male and female patients in two wings on either side of a central administration section. The facility's construction began in 1868, and was completed in 1871. It was designed by G. T. Hine, a notable asylum architect at the time, and was built with the concept that relaxing views and extreme isolation were beneficial to psychological recovery. This "enclosed community" plan called for staff living on the premises, only one access road, and its own rail line to the asylum.

In 1903, the East Sussex County Asylum (later named Hellingly Hospital) opened its doors to new patients. Although it was to be constructed quickly, things did not go as planned. The project's managers far exceeded its original schedule and budget; as a result, it remained partially completed for almost a quarter century after it first opened. The building closed in 2003 and was later seriously damaged in a 2007 fire. It is located on US 9 just north of Poughkeepsie. Sadly, this once glorious brick building has suffered a great deal. However, I was fortunate enough to make friends with more than a few photographers who supplied me with images of it.

Hudson River State Hospital. *Courtesy of Ken Schuler.*

EKG photo, Hudson River Hospital.
Courtesy of Ken Shuler.

Electrosurgical lobotomy photo,
Hudson River State Hospital.
Courtesy of Ken Shuler.

An operating room at Hudson River State Hospital. *Courtesy of Ken Shuler.*

Patients' records were often left behind at abandoned mental institutions, including the Hudson River State Hospital. *Courtesy of Ken Shuler.*

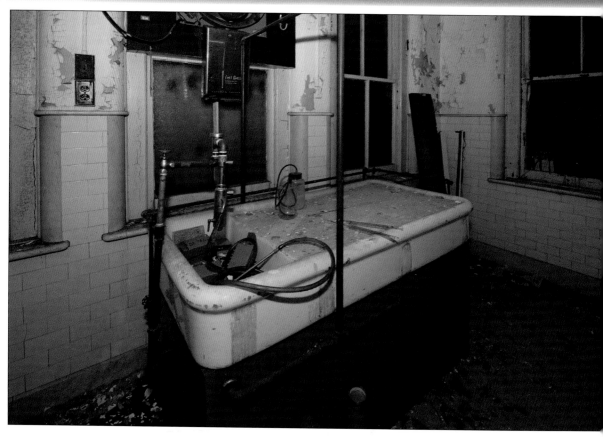

Autopsy photo, Hudson River State Hospital. *Courtesy of Ken Shuler.*

A view of the
room where
bodies from the
morgue were
kept in storage at
the Hudson River
State Hospital.
*Courtesy of Ken
Shuler.*

An abandoned office at the
Hudson River State Hospital.
Courtesy of Ken Shuler.

This stairway at Hudson
River State Hospital was
used by the administration.
Courtesy of Nan Guzauski.

The crumbling remains of the Hudson River State Hospital. *Courtesy of Nan Guzauski.*

These images offer a glimpse of what has become of this once historical structure.
Courtesy of Chandra Lampriech.

Kings Park Psychiatric Center

In 1885, the Kings County Farm housed the poor and mentally ill. The farm colony originally opened with fifty-five patients. As buildings were added, the number of patients increased as well. The asylum's overcrowding led to protest by the public and medical staff, which led to the state taking over in 1895. By 1900, the patient population had grown well over 2,000. It also had a staff of four hundred, more than one hundred permanent buildings, including a bakery, laundromat, amusement hall, bandstand, library, furniture repair shop, and nursing school. In 1954, Kings Park Psychiatric Center had over 9,000 patients. The Kirkbride had to be modernized as running water, fire escapes, and other new technologies were worked into building codes, making the basements a nightmarish maze of pipes and wires squeezing into the spaces of the old design. The central administration portion was still used, however, until around 2001, when the property went up for sale and was eventually sold to a developer.

New changes in treatment and the medical plan changing in America to "decentralize" psychiatric patients into community facilities or outpatient treatment later reduced the need for the hospital. All the patients were eventually moved out of the Kirkbride sometime around the mid-1970s, and the wards have since fallen into major disrepair. By the 1980s, KPPC was a shell of its former self; many buildings were abandoned, as it was forced to cut costs. By 1996, the Kings Park Psychiatric Center closed and its remaining patients were transferred to Pilgrim State. A story from one of the urban explorers claimed they encountered a girl after they entered a room, whose only exit door was locked. They said that the girl told them they didn't belong there and she screamed at them to leave the place. They tried the door and yelled back that the door was locked. Once more the girl screamed that they didn't belong and to leave and, with this, the door unlocked. As the explorers left, they looked back...the girl had vanished.

The property was bought by developers and was undergoing restoration, with plans to preserve the entire Kirkbride. However, in June 2007, lightning caused the male wing to catch fire, destroying much of this section of the building; as a result, the larger of the two wings is now a burned-out shell. The exterior walls have gaping holes that span two floors and the roof is missing in most parts. Restoration efforts have since halted.

Manteno State Hospital

With land purchased in 1927, the Manteno State Hospital opened its doors in the early 1930s. Like Bartonville State Hospital, Manteno was laid out in what was known as the cottage plan: patients were housed in a series of separate buildings rather than as in the Kirkbride design of one massive institution. When it first opened, Manteno accommodated 5,500 patients and 760 staff. Panic gripped the hospital in 1939, when 384 patients and staff came down with typhoid fever. *Time* magazine referred to the epidemic in an article titled "Manteno Madness" — forty-seven people died — as it reported: "Patients lay moaning in bed. Others, whipped by mad fear, beat against the screened windows, grappled with attendants… Every night kitchen boys and orderlies disappeared. Over 45 ran away in all."

If the Manteno Walls Could Talk...

Author's Note: The following is copied with permission by the author.

Personal feelings with some facts by author and radio host, Ed Shanahan

Well, they say at times you cannot tell the patients from the doctors in mental hospitals. Personally for me by reading the annual reports (I will mention what ones to read), it sounds like things were not right at this place. Many individuals in search of the paranormal — people who wander around the hallways and rooms of the buildings that are still standing — have stated hearing voices, crying, screaming, etc. and one individual refuses to go back after one location left negative feelings that would haunt her at night.

As you read some of the facts below, imagine what it may have been like. People mentally ill roaming the halls in a daze due to shock treatments, yelling and screaming all throughout the night, pounding on doors and walls. Therapy-like shock treatments, lobotomy, fever cabinets and who knows what else in the healing process of mental illness. No drugs as we know them today to control the problems many may have had. Not only did the patient have to live with what they had and the so-called treatments they were put through, but also everyone else in the same ward. I would imagine if you were not totally crazy going in, you may have been when coming out.

Over 8,000 patients at one time with a medical staff of only 200 plus. And the hospital was not made to house that many patients. Here is a bit of info from one of their annual reports: "At the present time we have twenty-seven graduate nurses on our staff, including the administrative, supervisory, and general duty nurses, which is eighteen less than at the same time a year ago."

From the Department of Public Health report: The nursing department was directed by a trained nurse, who was assisted by a number of supervisors all of whom were untrained lay persons. The registered nurses in the administrative plan took their orders from the lay supervisors, who, in turn, were responsible for contacting the staff physicians. The attendants in this department consisted of lay persons who also were responsible for nursing care.

Let's not forget one way of helping to heal the mentally ill — lobotomy — took America and some other countries by storm. They were performed in a wide scale in the 40s. Between 1939 and 1951, more than 18,000 lobotomies were performed in the United States. Even one of our famous U.S. Presidents, his sister had it done on her. Allegedly due to the father feeling he did not receive the respect from her that he demanded and received from his many other children (enough hints given on who the President was).

Here is a small list of things gone on there in one year (1941):

Male Intensive Therapy
Insulin - 87
Electric - 140
Fever Cabinet - 14
Metrazol - 10
Malaria – 31

Female Intensive Therapy
Insulin - 58
Electric - 55
Fever Cabinet - 10
Metrazol - 12

In 1983, the facility was authorized for closure by Governor James R. Thompson; it closed on December 31, 1985. After that, the Illinois Veterans home at Manteno was dedicated and still operates on a portion of the grounds of the original psychiatric facility. However, most of the rest of the facility's buildings have been demolished. Those that were abandoned were left in original condition. As of July 2009, many buildings have been renovated for other uses and a portion of the grounds is now the Manento Municipal Golf Course.

Normansfield Hospital

Originally a home, in 1868 a private facility caring for those with developmental disabilities and psychiatric issues named the "White House" was opened. This facility was intended just for the wealthy, but in time was expanded to accommodate more patients and became known as the Normansfield Training Institution for Imbeciles or, more politely, simply, the Normansfield Hospital. By the year 1896, the hospital had 160 patients.

As it turned out, the hospital's founder, John Langdon-Down, was a pioneer in the education and training of the handicapped and studied the characteristics of the conditions of his patients. Dr. Langdon-Down, using scientific classification, measured, photographed, and catalogued everything he studied and, when his patients died, he would do his own autopsies, during which he studied the deceased's brain matter. In 1866, Langdon Down classified a specific group of patients having oriental characteristics that he described as "Mongolian," which is where the phrase "Mongolian Idiot" came from. Much later, in 1965, the World Health Organization renamed this term "Down's Syndrome" at the request of international experts, as well as the People's Republic of Mongolia. Ironically, Langdon-Down's own grandson, born nine years after his death, had the very same condition, Down's Syndrome.

The hospital closed its doors in 1997; the land was sold to Laign Homes for housing in 1999, with a hotel in development, but the project was never completed. Today, some of the main hospital buildings remain empty.

North Hampton Lunatic Hospital

Located in Northampton, Massachusetts, an urban city located in the western part of the state, about a two-hour drive from Boston, this nineteenth century insane asylum quietly rests atop a hill. Built in 1856, the Northampton Lunatic Hospital was the fourth Kirkbride building to be constructed, this one to house 250 patients.

Visitors to this place claim to hear footsteps, whispers, and doors opening and closing. Sometimes, as when three friends entered the building one night through a window, they claim they heard the squeak of wheels...as if someone was pushing a wheelchair or gurney through the empty place. These friends also mentioned that there were uncountable amounts of rusted surgical utensils scattered across the floors in a room marked "Lobotomies." On the second floor, there were dirty, white padded rooms. A female member of the group recalls opening a random door to a room of pitch black darkness. Out of curiosity, she threw a rock into the darkness...only to never hear it land. She concludes her experiences with: "It was just scary as hell." Other patients were locked in these padded rooms and told to sit in the chair, for hours on end, while staff on the other side of the mirror watched and questioned them through an intercom. Once they thought they knew what was wrong with the patient, they would sometimes perform a lobotomy on them.

Infirmary wings were added to both sides in 1905, with frequent additions built since then; however, the hospital remained congested and the old structure was decaying quickly. After many additions to relieve overcrowding, the building had become a confusing maze of rooms and hallways. By the 1950s, the patient population had peaked at over 2,500; by 1961, more patients were being discharged than brought in, until it finally closed its doors in 1993. The Northampton State Hospital lived nearly two hundred years; today, the old buildings stand empty, the rooms silent witnesses to the horrors that took place there.

Hallway, North Hampton Lunatic Hospital. *Courtesy of Nan Guzauski.*

Northville Hospital

When Northville Hospital was built in the 1920s, it was considered to be Michigan's largest hospital complex. It was back in the 1920s that the state was given the power "to provide the care, custody, and maintenance of feebleminded persons within such country." The hospital was converted to a psychiatric facility in 1952, and then converted to the Wayne Co. Training School, known as the Wayne County Child Development Center, and the hospital permanently closed its doors. In 1978, the remaining caretakers were laid-off and the property was completely abandoned by the early 1980s.

In the mid-1980s, several fires gutted many of the areas, and locals began to explore the underground tunnels, with the intrepid explorers claiming to have seen evidence of supposed "satanic cults operating down there. We would come across bones and blood and pentagrams."

More vandalizing of the main buildings followed. The campus began to be called the "Northville Tunnels" by these teenaged visitors. The 1990s saw a proposed housing development to be built on the property and, in 1998, the eventual demolition was well under way for redevelopment of the property into a huge golf course.

Norwich State Hospital

In October 1904, located in Norwich, Connecticut, stands the remains of the mental health facility initially created for the mentally ill and those found guilty of crimes by insanity originally established as Norwich State Hospital for the Insane. The years 1907 through 1995 saw an additional thirteen structures built, including a laboratory and other structures.

Spanning hundreds of acres of property, the buildings were connected by a series of underground passageways that were often used to transport patients from one area to another. It was speculated that these areas were locations used for the torture of patients who became uncontrollable. Now, however, the tunnels have become a means by which urban explorers enter the grounds of the hospital undetected by the security officers who have been hired by the state to patrol the abandoned facility. In 1996, when Norwich State Hospital was closed, the State Department of Public Works became responsible for the property and its remaining patients were transferred to Connecticut Valley Hospital.

Norwich is listed on both the state and national register of historic places for its architectural and historical significance and, thus, many of the buildings, grounds, and infrastructure cannot be removed. It is interesting to note that former staff and other witnesses claim the spot to be haunted and a paranormal investigating team even explored the location for the television show *Ghost Hunters*.

Norwich State Hospital in Preston, Connecticut. *Courtesy of Chandra Lampreich.*

Norwich State Hospital in Preston, Connecticut.
Courtesy of Chandra Lampreich.

Norwich State Hospital in Preston, Connecticut.
Courtesy of Chandra Lampreich.

Norwich State Hospital in Preston, Connecticut.
Courtesy of Chandra Lampreich.

This ward is where the more violent patients were kept at Norwich State Hospital. *Courtesy of Ken Shuler.*

A birdcage is seen inside the "Violent Ward" at Norwich State Hospital.
Courtesy of Ken Shuler.

The tunnels at Norwich State Hospital.
Courtesy of Ken Shuler.

Theater, Norwich State Hospital. *Courtesy of Ken Shuler*.

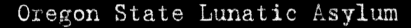

Oregon State Lunatic Asylum

The Oregon State Lunatic Asylum is the oldest asylum in the Western United States, built in 1883 on Asylum Avenue in the capital city of Salem. This foreboding and deteriorating asylum is the oldest of its kind still in operation on the West Coast. A total of seventy buildings are scattered across the campus, all constructed between 1883 and the mid-1950s. In January 2008, the United States Department of Justice threatened a massive lawsuit if the inhumane conditions endured by the patients there were not ceased. Among other things, the Department of Justice deemed that the conditions at the asylum abhorrently infringed upon the constitutional rights of the patients.

In March 2008, the entire 125-year-old, 144-acre psychiatric facility was added to the National Register of Historic Places. Interestingly, it was also the filming location in 1976 for the Academy Award-winning, cinematic cult classic, *One Flew Over the Cuckoo's Nest*, starring Jack Nicholson. The largest, oldest, and most famous structure within the institution is the J Building — it was this building that served as the location for virtually all of the interior movie scenes.

Now renamed Oregon State Hospital, the hospital peaked in the late 1950s and has slowly declined in the number of patients they take in; however, it continues to house 650 "lunatics" or, if you will, people with severe mental illness and the allegations of abuse and atrocious conditions persist to this day. The Oregon State Government wanted to demolish the J Building in 1988 due to life-threatening health and safety dangers posed to patients and staff. There is an abundance of lead-based paint and asbestos throughout the building. Urns containing the ashes of unclaimed patients still remain there as well.

Pennhurst State School and Asylum

Pennhurst State School and Asylum, originally known as the Eastern Pennsylvania State Institution for the Feeble-Minded and Epileptic, is located at the edge of Chester County in Pennsylvania. Built in 1903 as an institution for the mentally and physically disabled individuals of Southeastern Pennsylvania, when the Pennsylvania Legislature authorized the creation of a commission to take charge of the care of the thousands of "feeble-minded persons in insane hospitals," it was decided to place them in a reformatory for specialized institutional care. The massive 54,000-square-foot building was two stories and made of red brick, terra cotta, and granite. They were connected by fire-proof tunnels, with walkways on top of the tunnels for transporting residents and a parallel steam piping system, on the 1,400-acre campus in the cottage plan formation.

Much later the hospital superintendent reported to the Board of Trustees that "it is without question absolutely wrong to place the feeble-minded and epileptic in the same institution. They are not the same; they are as different, one from the other, as day is from night. They are mentally, physically and morally incompatible, and require entirely different treatment."

In 1913, the legislature appointed a Commission for the Care of the Feeble-Minded, which stated, "The disabled were unfit for citizenship and posed a menace to the peace, and thus recommended a program of custodial care. Furthermore, the Commission desired to prevent the intermixing of the genes of those imprisoned with the general population." Pennhurst's Chief Physician quoted Henry H. Goddard, a leading eugenicist, stating: "Every feeble-minded person is a potential criminal. The general public, although more convinced today than ever before that it is a good thing to segregate the idiot or the distinct imbecile, they have not as yet been convinced as to the proper treatment of the defective delinquent, which is the brighter and more dangerous individual."

Pennhurst Hospital. *Courtesy of Chandra Lampriech.*

As time passed, public complaints and a class-action lawsuit filed by Pennhurst employees alleged abuse against Pennhurst State School. It was presided over by U.S. District Judge Raymond J. Broderick in 1977, and the institution was found guilty of violating patients' constitutional rights.

In 1968, conditions at Pennhurst were exposed in a five-part television news report anchored by local NBC10 correspondent Bill Baldini, called "Suffer the Little Children." Also, the case of Halderman v. Pennhurst State School & Hospital, 446 F.Supp. 1295 (E.D. Pa., 1977), asserted that the mentally disabled also have a constitutional right to living quarters and education. Terry Lee Halderman had been a resident of Pennhurst and, upon her release, she filed suit in the district court on behalf of herself and other residents of Pennhurst. The complaint alleged that

Exterior and interior views of Pennhurst Hospital. *Courtesy of Chandra Lampriech.*

conditions at Pennhurst were unsanitary, inhumane, and dangerous, violating the fourteenth amendment, and that Pennhurst used cruel and unusual punishment in violation of the eighth and fourteenth amendments, as well as the Pennsylvania Mental Health and Retardation Act of 1966 (MH/MR). While the District Court agreed that certain of the patients' rights had been violated, the case was eventually overturned at the U.S. Supreme Court, which found that the federal courts cannot order state officials to comply with state laws, due to the eleventh amendment. It was ordered that Pennhurst State School close by 1987. The deinstitutionalization process began and would last several years. Nearly 460 patients were discharged or transferred to other facilities; the judge had mandated that Pennhurst was responsible for discussing treatment plans with each patients' family to decide what would be best for the patient.

By 2005, Pennhurst was sold to a private developer, Pennhurst Associates, for $2 million. The Pennhurst Memorial and Preservation Alliance was formed to advocate for making use of the site. During the last decade, there have been numerous claims of paranormal activity occurring at the grounds of the Pennhurst property. These range from seeing children playing on broken down playground equipment, ghostly apparitions passing by windows, faint screams, and disembodied voices. Shore Paranormal Research Society was asked to come in and try to debunk these claims. Over numerous visits to the site, members of the group had countless personal experiences, including EVPs and seeing shadow apparitions. They concluded that there is a high level of paranormal activity at the complex.

Interior views of Pennhurst Hospital.
Courtesy of Chandra Lampriech.

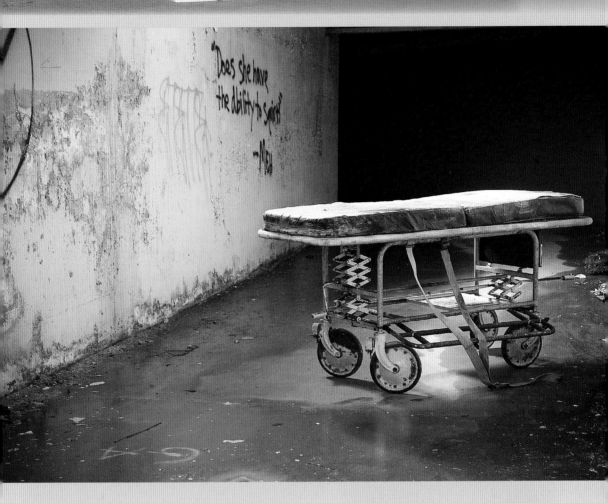

Philadelphia State Hospital (Byberry

This enormous complex started out as a small work farm for the mentally handicapped in Byberry back in 1906. By the mid-1920s, the buildings included administrative offices, treatment areas, patient housing, chapels, a theater, and a morgue, as well as several dormitories, an infirmary, several kitchens, laundry, and two coal power plants.

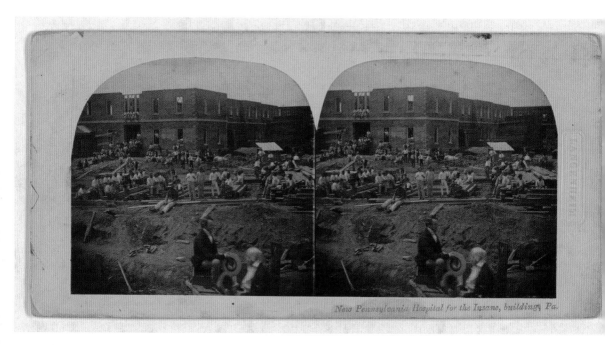

Philadelphia State Hospital for the Insane. *Courtesy of Library of Congress.*

The Philadelphia Hospital for Mental Diseases opened its doors to its first patient in 1907. Its population quickly grew, but so too did the stories of abuse and neglect. Governor Edward Martin inspected Byberry on August 24, 1946. Due to lack of funds, the asylum had quickly fallen into disrepair. Patients wound up sleeping in hallways, and raw sewage was found on the bathroom floors during an inspection of the facility. Many patients were forced to live huddled in small and filthy rooms with no social interaction or supervision. Byberry became known as a "real life house of horrors," as murder, suicide, and brutality reigned. During World War II, some 3,000 conscientious objectors who refused to fight because of their religious beliefs, were sent to work at state mental hospitals across the country. These individuals were shocked witnesses to the conditions of the hospitals. Two objectors, Charlie Lord and Warren Sawyer, were assigned to Byberry and wrote detailed letters home about the horror at Byberry and in other state hospitals. Lords even snuck in a camera, concealing it in his coat pocket. His photographs were shown to Eleanor Roosevelt in September 1945, which led to reform campaigns, and also health officials and journalists. In May 1946, they were published in a *Life* magazine article entitled "Bedlam 1946" and a 1948 *New York Times* article "Herded Like Cattle." Albert Deutch's 1948 publication, *Shame of the States*, also detailed these conditions.

By the 1960s, Philadelphia State Hospital consisted of more than fifty buildings, 7,000 patients, and eight hundred staff members. Deinstitutionalization took place in the1980s. Horrid living conditions were once again publicized after an investigation of patient abuse, this time involving sexual exploitation and starvation. The hospital was closed in June 1990, after which Byberry was cannibalized by salvagers stealing copper.

In 1991, the hospital was slated for demolition, which did not happen due to an estimated $16 million removal cost of asbestos that was found inside, thus the buildings have been left to rot. The remaining ruins have been torched and sprayed with graffiti by local juveniles by the dozens, according to local police. Over time, portions of the property were sold and redeveloped for commercial and industrial purposes or will be demolished for a housing development.

Pilgrim State Hospital

Also known as Pilgrim Psychiatric Center, the hospital opened on October 1, 1931, with 825 acres and a population of one hundred patients that were transferred from the Central Islip Psychiatric Center. It is named for Dr. Charles W. Pilgrim, who was the Commissioner of Mental Health in the early 1900s. Nine months after it opened, Pilgrim was caring for 2,018 patients. In 1954, Pilgrim's population hit its peek of 13,875 patients. After this, just like the other psychiatric hospitals, the population began to decrease.

Pilgrim was the largest facility of its kind in the world when it was built. The hospital was self-sufficient, in that it had its own water works, electric light plant, heating plant, sewage system, police and fire department, courts, church, post office, cemetery, laundry facilities, as well as grew its own food. Today Pilgrim Psychiatric Center remains in operation as one of the last of the large farm colonies on Long Island. Its history is well-known for its tragic violations of human rights, with the endless cases of mistreatment of patients, who were forced to undergo electroshock therapy and lobotomies. Other scandals have originated here as well, allegedly worse than the ones that surround other institutions of this caliber. In 1996, an article in the *New York Times* declared the treatment of patients at Pilgrim "unconstitutional."

However, it was only in the year 2000 that *Newsday* exposed the institution for all of the investigations of deaths that occurred there. The place is silent, as invaders walk through the empty rooms, with only the rusted old bed frames, dressers, and medical equipment amidst the debris. Pilgrim's morgue was no disappointment. It had sixteen body freezers from floor to ceiling, complete with the table on which the autopsies were performed. Above this table, painted on the wall, was the quote: "Let conversations cease. Let laughter flee. This is the place where death delights to help the living." I discovered it was a motto posted on the wall of the autopsy room of Dr. Milton Helpern, the medical examiner of New York City in the 1960s.

Also, it is said to be haunted due to the rumor that Pilgrim is were serial killer Ted Bundy killed a coed in the catacombs of tunnels under nearby Sackett Hall at Oregon State University.

Riverside Hospital
(North Brother Island)

Constructed in 1885, North Brother Island is home to a series of crumbling Gothic buildings. It once housed Riverside Hospital and is dubbed the creepiest island in New York City. The Brother Islands, as they are often called, are located in the East River, between Queens and the Bronx. The facility treated various diseases, such as smallpox, typhoid, tuberculosis, measles, and scarlet fever. Many patients from the Renwick Smallpox Hospital on Roosevelt Island were relocated to North Brother once the new facility was built. A ferry located at 132nd Street in the Bronx transported staff, patients, and supplies to the island, yet it remained very isolated — it did not even have telegraph lines until as late as 1894. The hospital had about 1,200 people in quarantine during an 1892 typhus outbreak.

The most infamous patient to reside at Riverside might be Mary Mallon, also known as "Typhoid Mary." A carrier of typhoid, Mary had the disease, but showed no apparent signs of the illness — yet she was quite capable of spreading it. She worked as a cook at various places in Manhattan and Long Island between the years 1900 and 1907, where she transmitted the infection to as many as fifty-three people. As they got sick or died, she would find employment elsewhere. Soon, Mary was questioned by health officials. Her response was that she did not believe she had the disease and adamantly refused to cooperate. In 1907, Mary was taken into custody by police officers and the Health Department gave her an ultimatum — either have her gall bladder removed (where typhoid carrier germs lived) or be exiled to North Brother Island. She refused the surgical operation, which was risky and unpredictable at the time, and was committed to Riverside Hospital, where she lived out the rest of her life in an isolated cottage on the island. She began working at the hospital in 1918, becoming a nurse and finally a laboratory assistant. Mary suffered a stroke in 1933 and remained bedridden at Riverside until she died on November 11, 1938.

Riverside Hospital was permanently shut down in 1963 due to a staff corruption scandal, leaving the entire island abandoned. It is currently off-limits to the public and patrolled often due to the proximity of a nearby prison complex on Rikers Island.

Riverside State Hospital for the Insane.
Courtesy of Library of Congress.

Royal Hope Hospital

The Royal Hope Hospital, or as it is also referred to "Our Lady of Gaudalupe," stood in the very same spot from 1784 to 1821; but the actual building now located on the property at 3 Avilles Street, St. Augustine, Florida, is not the original structure. The building that stands there today is a replica of the original.

The original old Military hospital had operated on the dying from the Seminole and Civil wars, and is located near the Spanish Quarter Village in Old St. Augustine. City officials found piles and piles of bones believed to be a Timucuan Indian burial site when they dug up the foundation to work on the waterlines under the old hospital. People believe the new building built there is still haunted by the souls of the original hospital and the disturbed Native Americans. Visitors to the Spanish Military Hospital Museum (built on the property for tourists) often experience strange occurrences and have had many sightings of a real ghost.

These same visitors also told stories of the actual sick beds moving across the room and bumping into their legs, drink cans sliding across benches placed outside for their convenience, and the haunting sounds of footsteps in an empty upstairs area. In the surgeon's room, tourists can see displays of medical tools and other information regarding hospitals from that era. In this room, commonly reported are the many strange sounds heard and the objects that seem to move or shake of their own volition. In another room, called the Apothecary, where only staff members were allowed in order to dispense medicine, many have reported seeing shadows moving strangely across the walls and hearing the sobbing of some unseen man.

Paranormal experts from across the United States have said this is a real hotbed of haunted Florida spirit and paranormal activity. Most experts agree that these types of hauntings tend to occur in areas where human emotion is or was concentrated on a regular basis. Orbs, which are believed to be a manifest of the spirit world, have been captured in photographs.

St. John's Asylum

An abandoned asylum with an imposing water tower, St. John's in Lincolnshire also features a freshly restored facade — though the interior is another story. Opened in 1852 based on a design by John R. Hamilton, the hospital was originally built to house 250 inmates, but was enlarged at later dates.

St. John's was shut down in 1989 and bought by developers who have converted half of the site into houses, but the main asylum buildings are Grade II listed and cannot be demolished. The interior, however, is little more than a shell. Practically every room is stripped bare, although the Y-shaped stairwell remains of interest; so too the extremely cramped cells lining the long, barren corridors. The grounds of St. John's formerly had their own cemetery together with chapel and mortuary, now no more.

Saint Mary's Asylum

St. Mary's Asylum in Northumberland lies in an isolated location yet with several access routes to its chapel, superintendent's residence, and main entrance. Its compact arrow plan was the work of G. T. Hine and is not unlike that of Hellingly, which he also designed in a similarly red-brick style. Opened in 1914, St. Mary's was soon commandeered during World War One; then, after the modification of the isolation hospital to form a sanatorium for TB patients, it was again used through World War Two. Despite various proposals for redeveloping St. Mary's, today this relic from a bygone era of mental health treatment is disused apart from a few occupied staff residences. The Grade II listed buildings have remained in remarkably good condition, probably because of their remote location, though the boiler house chimney has collapsed due to structural failure and its emergency medical huts were demolished prior to the hospital's closure in 1995. Most of the equipment has now been taken from inside, but not all.

Saint Michael's State Hospital

Founded in 1892 by the Sisters of St. Joseph to care for the sick and the poor of Toronto's inner city, this Catholic hospital is said to be haunted by Sister Vincenza, or "Vinnie," who died in the 1950s. Staff and patients alike have claimed to see lights turning on and off and blankets being pulled up over those dozing in their beds in one of the wards on the seventh floor.

Severalls Hospital

This 300-acre property, started from a design by Frank Whitmore, was the second Essex County asylum. Opened in 1913 to relieve pressure from the Warley Asylum, the design is based on the "Echelon Plan," with buildings linked to one another by a network of interconnecting corridors. It housed some 2,000 patients.

Diana Gittins wrote in her book, *Madness in Its Place: Narratives of Severalls Hospital, 1913-1997*, that often women were admitted by their own family, sometimes as the result of bearing illegitimate children or if they had been subjected to rape. The book also quotes a nurse who worked at Severalls from 1936: "You know the corridors? There were lots of little ladies scrubbing the corridors. They would be scrubbing the corridors with sack aprons on their knees. Have they got windows in there now? Well, there never used to be any windows. Open to the elements! And we'd come off duty and all you'd here was screaming — the bats would be coming up and down the corridors! Yes! They'd be flying up and down the corridors! When we came off duty we'd put our capes over our heads and we'd be screaming!"

Most of the structures were built in an unembellished, typically Edwardian style, and those still standing have changed little since the hospital's closure in 1997. Like so many others, its buildings have suffered vandalism and fire, leading to the demolition of the charred main hall in 2007. It still holds leftover medical equipment and a mortuary containing body refrigerators.

Severalls Asylum, in
Colchester, United
Kingdom. *Courtesy of
Chandra Lampreich.*

Staten Island Infirmary

Erected in 1809, the castle-shaped infirmary located on Staten Island was its first fully functioning hospital. In a report dated in 1868, the total number of patients was eighty-eight, of which fifty-seven of them where listed "cured." By 1890, the hospital's funds had grown, along with the need to accommodate a larger amount of people. For the third time, the Infirmary moved to a six-acre site on Castleton Avenue in New Brighton. By the end of that first year in its new location, the Infirmary treated 346 inpatients and six hundred outpatients, some of which were soldiers that were wounded in the Spanish-American War.

In 1913, the infirmary officially changed its name to the Staten Island Hospital. After its closure in the late 1970s, a few people tried to renovate the hospital by converting it into condominiums. Although interior construction was nearly finished, no one was interested in residing there and the buildings remain empty to all but the animals, homeless, and drug addicts. There have been reports of howls and other noises coming from the building, as well as lights seen in windows.

Staten Island Infirmary, 1887.
Courtesy of Library of Congress.

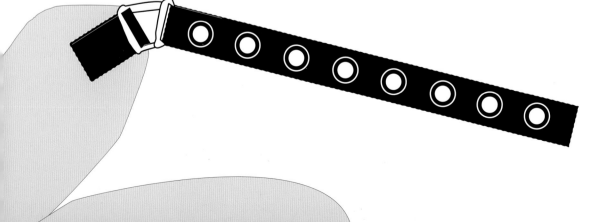

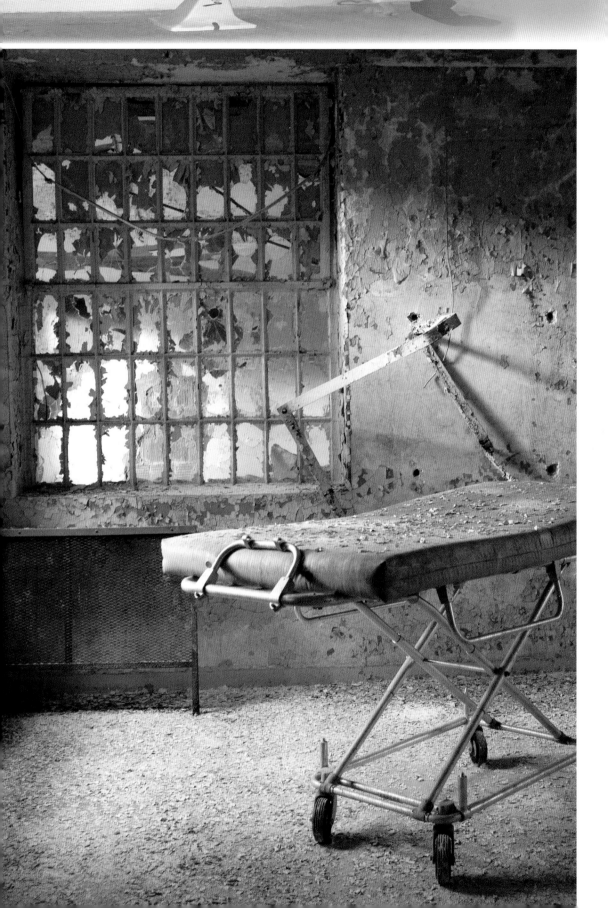

Taunton State Hospital

Taunton State Hospital, formerly known as the State Lunatic Hospital at Taunton, is a psychiatric hospital. Built in 1854 in Taunton, Massachusetts, it was designed by the architect Elbridge Boyden, using the style of the Kirkbride Hospital Plan. One of its most beautiful features was its breezeways, which were added in the 1890s to connect the end of the wards to the hospital's infirmary buildings. While doing research for this book, I read on a forum for asylums that axe murderess Lizzie Borden was treated here, but little evidence can be found to support that claim.

Elizabeth Graham, a *Taunton Gazette* writer, reported: "Rumors of malignant supernatural activity surround Taunton State Hospital, which began housing the insane and mentally ill in the

mid-1850s. The Goss building, which is still in use, reportedly is home to, among various other spirits, the ghost of a man in white who appears on the third floor. At night, banging, screams, and moans can supposedly be heard from the woods behind the hospital. Some believe the sounds are made by the ghosts of patients."

In 1975, the hospital was abandoned. In 1999, the large dome, which towered over the hospital's administration, collapsed. Five years later, on the night of March 19, 2006, a massive fire broke out in the center of the building, which included the administration and theater. Afterwards, these damaged parts were leveled, leaving only the wings. In 2009, workers began a complete demolition of the disused buildings on the property.

Taunton State Hospital in Taunton, Massachusetts.
Courtesy of Chandra Lampreich.

The tunnels at Taunton State Hospital. *Courtesy of Nan Guzauski.*

Taunton State Hospital in a partial collapse state. *Courtesy of Nan Guzauski.*

One of the examination rooms where patients were likely experimented on, Taunton State Hospital. *Courtesy of Nan Guzauski.*

Trans-Allegheny Lunatic Asylum

Construction started in Weston, West Virginia, in 1858 on the future state psychiatric hospital using prison labor. Eventually, skilled European stonemasons were hired to complete the building. In 1861, during the Civil War, construction was interrupted for almost a year. Patients started arriving in 1864, though the asylum was not completely finished until 1881. This enormous 242,000-square-foot building was built on 666 acres for 250 patients, but by 1950 it held over 2,400. The hospital was renamed Weston State Hospital in 1913.

Records indicate frequent assaults, and worse, occurring. Patients killed other patients. Female employees were violated. A nurse who had gone missing was found nearly two months later…dead at the bottom of a never-used stairway. People visiting have reported hearing the

Trans Allegheny Lunatic Asylum.
Courtesy of Chandra Lampreich.

sound of gurneys being pushed up and down the hallways and, from the electroshock treatment rooms, faint screams. Apparitions and voices have reportedly been seen and heard all around the facility, with the majority of it occurring on the fourth floor, which was where wounded Civil War soldiers were treated.

In 1990, the hospital was designated a historical landmark. In 2007, it was bought during an auction. The new owners officially changed the name back to its original name, the Trans-Allegheny Lunatic Asylum, and the place is now open for tours. A year later, when the television show TAPS (The Atlantic Paranormal Society) was invited to investigate the place for evidence of the paranormal, they said they heard a female laugh and banging noises. A representative from the show, Grant Wilson, also claimed there was an apparition standing in a corner "being sucked out of the room."

Traverse City State Hospital (Northern Michigan Asylum for the Insane)

Built in 1885, Traverse City State Hospital opened as the Northern Michigan Asylum for the Insane. The hospital's original theme was "beauty is therapy." Dr. James Decker Munson, hospital superintendent, felt that if people were surrounded by beauty and tranquility, a lot of their mental problems would cease to exist. For that reason, he did not allow the use of straightjackets. Following the model of the building's designer, Thomas Kirkbride, Traverse State Hospital was one of several Kirkbride buildings constructed in Michigan; Traverse City is the last in existence.

However, this tranquil and beautiful place still earned its reputation of being haunted since the hospital's closing in 1989. The mint green lead paint is peeling in the long corridors, forgotten furniture is in disarray, and the occasional graffiti is found on its vacant walls. Many of the porches are surrounded with metal grating, giving the appearance of animal cages. By the year 2004, some of the buildings that once housed the mentally ill were being transformed into condominiums, office space, and even a restaurant.

This former patient's room was typical of the patient housing at Traverse City and other institutions. *Courtesy of Wayne Overla.*

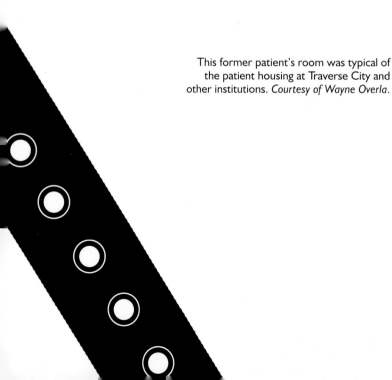

I ran across a story about a local Traverse City reporter's experience at the hospital. Working for the local news station, the reporter was taping a police officer during a story about teenage vandalism and destruction of property. He said, "When I was recording with a video camera, I got some loud and very spooky voices. When I edited the tape, I could hear the following. The voices said, 'Get out Now!' … 'Leave now or you will be sorry!' … 'Watch out Mike!' The scary thing is the officer's name was Mike! It was like the spirit was talking to us in real time! Sadly I tried to find this video in our company's archives, but failed. You should have been there! Me, the policeman, and the cam dude were freaking out."

This is not the only mention of occurrences, as there have been claims of various ghosts wandering the grounds of the hospital, echoing from the psychiatric wards. Apparitions of children and elderly people have also been reported to appear and disappear throughout. What will become of the place in the end is uncertain.

Trenton State Hospital
(New Jersey State Lunatic Asylum)

New Jersey State Lunatic Asylum was founded in 1848 by Dorthea Dix. This New Jersey State Psychiatric Hospital has an especially wretched history. Henry Cotton, the 1916 superintendent of the Trenton State Hospital in New Jersey, believed psychosis was caused by "chronic pus infections" and treated sufferers not only with tooth removal, but also mutilated patients by removing limbs, the stomach, large intestine, tonsils, uterus, and colon. A 1924 study revealed that forty-three percent of Cotton's patients had died, and that he had killed more than one hundred people with his intestinal surgeries alone. Long after his departure, the hospital continued with the practice of dental extractions right up to 1960. Although a number of buildings on its campus are in disuse, parts of the hospital operate to this day.

Patient room, Trenton State Hospital. *Courtesy of Ken Shuler.*

A gurney in the hallway of the abandoned Trenton State Hospital. *Courtesy of Ken Schuler.*

Laughing gas was one method of treatment, Trenton State Hospital. *Courtesy of Ken Schuler.*

Dental tools, Trenton State Hospital. *Courtesy of Ken Schuler.*

Hallway, Trenton State Hospital. *Courtesy of Ken Shuler.*

Hallway, Trenton State Hospital. *Courtesy of Nan Guzauski.*

Trenton State Hospital.
Courtesy of Nan Guzauski.

Patient room, Trenton
State Hospital. *Courtesy
of Nan Guzauski.*

Undercliff Sanitorium

In the early 1900s through the 1940s, a sanatorium where children with diseases like German measles, rubella, and mumps were brought to die was established. Undercliff is now an abandoned building that is host to many different ghostly apparitions. Visitors to its property say that they can hear children crying and laughing, coming from the old brick building that still stands to this day. Eyewitnesses claim to see former patients in the windows...only to vanish. A young patient who was murdered by a group of other patients with plastic utensils is said to walk along the old courtyard amid barely discernable screams coming from rooms where shock therapy was supposedly administered.

Waverly Hills Sanatorium

With a death tally as high as 64,000 patients who were ravaged by a deadly disease commonly referred to as the "white death" or tuberculosis, which quickly wiped out entire towns, the Waverly Hills Sanatorium in Louisville, Kentucky, is believed to be the most haunted place in the country. In 1926, a hospital was constructed on a windswept hill in southern Jefferson County that had been designed to combat this horrific disease. However, it was poorly chosen to be constructed on swampland, and so the location did nothing but increase the disease despite the fact it was considered the most advanced hospital of its kind in the world. Still, at the time, not much was known about the disease and how to treat it, so a lot of the treatments were extremely experimental.

The majority of patients left through what came to be known as the "body chute," which was a tunnel that led from the hospital to railroad tracks that allowed for discreet corpse disposal. This elaborate system was a motorized rail and cable system by which the bodies were lowered in secret to the waiting trains at the bottom of the hill, in order that patients would not see it and become demoralized.

Various methods were used as treatment, some of which consisted of having the lungs exposed to ultraviolet light to try and stop the spread of the disease, in what was known as "sun rooms," on the roof or open porches of the hospital. Combined with the belief that fresh air was thought to also be the cure, patients were often placed out on open porches — photographs show patients lounging in chairs covered with snow. Another, even worse treatment, described as a "last resort," was a ghastly procedure where balloons were implanted in the lungs and then filled with air to expand them after operations in which the patients' muscles and ribs were removed in order to allow the lungs to expand further and let in more oxygen.

Back view of Waverly Hills' TB ward. *Courtesy of Tim Shaw.*

Front entrance of the TB ward at Waverly Hills. *Courtesy of Tim Shaw.*

Budget cuts from the 1960s to the 1970s led to both horrible conditions and mistreatment of patients and, by 1982, the state closed the facility. The buildings and property were auctioned off, yet changed ownership repeatedly over the next several decades. As time passed, Waverly Hills later attracted both the homeless seeking shelter, and juvenile delinquents, who broke in and started rumors of Waverly Hills being haunted by ghosts. Stories speak of a hearse that appeared in the back of the building dropping off coffins and a woman with bleeding wrists who cried for help, among others. It is said that a ghostly child haunts the third floor, as people report having heard a ball bouncing on the floor and down the stairs. Also, faint voices of children are often heard chanting "Ring-a-round-the-Rosie" up on the roof.

The Waverly is also famous for the story of two nurses who committed suicide there: In 1928, the head nurse was found dead in Room 502 after hanging herself from the light fixture; in 1932, another nurse who worked in Room 502 was said to have jumped from the roof patio and plunged several stories to her death. My friend, the Reverend Tim Shaw, who visited here several times, told me of people who have seen her full body apparition on this floor and that ghost researchers are drawn to the fifth floor, where the two nurses' stations were and where the nurses committed suicide.

The Louisville Ghost Hunters Society held two ghost conferences there, presenting the hospital to a national television audience. Historical and paranormal tours are given for a $20 donation, but must be reserved ahead of time.

The body chute can be seen inside Waverly Hills' TB ward. *Courtesy of Tim Shaw.*

Autopsy table, Waverly Hills. *Courtesy of Tim Shaw.*

Morgue, Waverly Hills. *Courtesy of Tim Shaw.*

Waverly Hills TB Ward cafeteria.

Waverly Hills TB Ward Patient Rooms.

Waverly Hills TB Ward Door that would not open — axe hits.

Waverly Hills TB Ward nurses station.

All images courtesy of Tim Shaw.

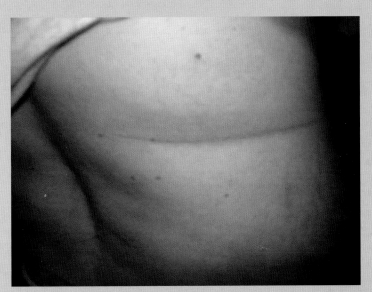

A Waverly Hills TB Ward investigator receives a mystery scratch.

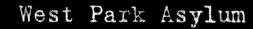

West Park Asylum

Designed by William C. Clifford-Smith and opened in 1923 after use during World War Two, West Park Asylum in Surrey is a sprawling complex of red-brick buildings that radiate out of a now destroyed central hall. It was the last in a long legacy of psychiatric hospitals in London, which in its heyday housed up to 2,000 patients. In the mid-1990s, the hospital fell into neglect and, by the year 2003, it closed its doors. West Park is now derelict, and its impressive buildings, extensive boiler houses, and plant rooms are slowly decaying. Former patients' belongings can still be seen, as well as the various hospital equipment and padded cells.

West Park Asylum.
Courtesy of Dawid Jaguia

Padded cell, West Park Asylum. *Courtesy of Dawid Jagusiak.*

Wernersville State Hospital

Wernersville, located right outside of Reading, Pennsylvania, in Berks County, is still in use as a treatment center. Other facilities were added to the complex, including a full kitchen, dining room, chapel, infirmary, employees' cafeteria, bake shop, boiler house, laundry, ice plant, filtration plant, and farm buildings. In the late 1890s, a small railroad station was built adjacent to the hospital. The Pennsylvania General Assembly authorized the creation of the State Asylum for the Chronic Insane back in June 22, 1891. The facility was to be a public mental hospital for persons needing extended care. Courts were not permitted to make direct admissions to Wernersville; only patients who had at least one year of care at another state mental hospital were eligible for admission. The older patients talk about the headless orderly and a lady who died ninety years ago that walks around the grounds with a doll amid the unmarked cemetery and an abandon building on the grounds. Many deaths at the hospital were attributed to the staff by way of neglect and abuse, as the visiting physicians treated the patients as "guinea pigs" to evaluate what to do with patients at their own hospitals. At last report, Wernersville will be bankrupt and closed by the year 2013.

Willard Psychiatric Hospital

A 2007 *New York Times* story on this abandoned psychiatric center in the Finger Lakes region of New York mentioned forgotten trunks and suitcases found in an attic. A total of 427 suitcases, trunks, crates, and bundles were discovered after the hospital shut down in 1995. Penn State's Paranormal Research Society (PRS) team spent time at Willard Psychiatric Hospital in upstate New York during the first season of *Paranormal States*, during which executive producer George Plamondon said, "Are they imagining it, or are they real? That's part of what PRS is trying to find out." The PRS team, led by president Ryan Buell, used special equipment to try to measure and document sounds and temperature changes to see if any spirits might be discovered. As a consultant on one of their shows, I happened to not only be friends with Eilfie Music, but also a longtime friend of the show's guest psychic, Michelle Belanger, both of whom assured me they encountered the presence of the deceased in many locations they film at.

Prone to the typical electroshock treatments, ice baths, and insulin shocks that were so common in that era, nearly half of the 54,000 patients who lived at Willard during its 126-year existence died there. In one case reported during the Depression, a French woman, who was thirty-six years old in 1932, can be seen in photos spanning her forty-seven years there drastically change as she was prescribed the first generation of neuroleptic drugs, which caused an incurable movement disorder. A photograph from around 1960 shows her face frozen into a tight frown, with the accompanying doctor's note describing her "shriveled, wizened face, narrow eyes" and a "stiff and sarcastic smile frozen on her face." Ironically it was the institution that caused her situation and misdiagnosis.

These restraints can be seen at the Willard Psychiatric Hospital.
Courtesy of Nan Guzauski.

Patient room, Willard Psychiatric Hospital. *Courtesy of Nan Guzauski.*

The Beauty Shop, Willard Psychiatric Hospital. *Courtesy of Nan Guzauski.*

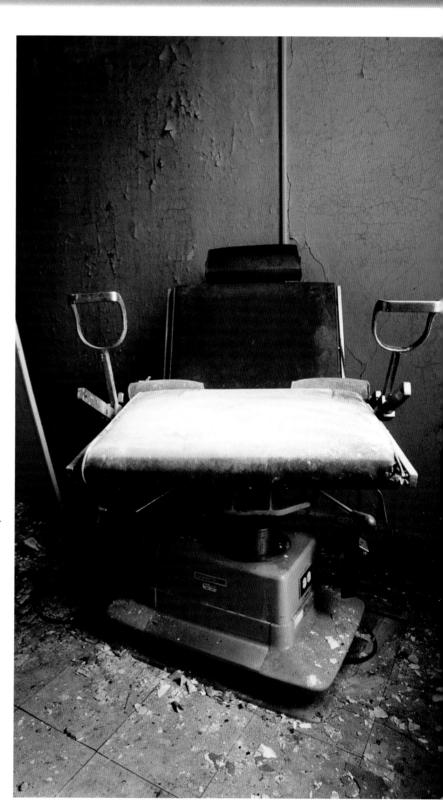

Examination room, Willard Psychiatric Hospital. *Courtesy of Nan Guzauski.*

Willowbrook State School

Located in the Willowbrook neighborhood of Staten Island in New York City until 1987, the New York State Department of Mental Hygiene opened its facility there in October 1947. The institution was named Willowbrook State School, a state-supported institution for children with mental retardation. Designed for 4,000 it buckled under the strain of a population of 6,000 by 1965.

During its first decade of operation, nearly all of the children developed hepatitis, primarily hepatitis A, due to the fact that in 1966 medical researcher Saul Krugman conducted a medical study there in which healthy children were intentionally given an injection of the virus and then monitored to gauge the effects of the treatment combating it. Krugman was forced to discontinue his study after people found out. The public also found out how New York City's mentally disabled children, abandoned there by their families or sent there by foster care agencies, suffered in the overcrowded, filthy living conditions and negligent treatment. By 1965, Willowbrook was both the biggest state-run institution for the mentally handicapped — and one of the worst. Its deplorable conditions and questionable medical practices and experiments, combined with public outcry, eventually led to its closure in 1987, after legislation began protecting the civil rights of the handicapped.

Later, many of the facility's buildings were incorporated into the campus of the College of Staten Island in the early 1990s. The rest of the buildings sit abandoned and are falling to ruin in the Staten Island Greenbelt. Sen. Robert Kennedy toured the institution in 1966, proclaiming it a "snake pit" and that "Willowbrook State School was not even fit for animals to live in." In 1972, Geraldo Rivera, in his early days as an investigative reporter for the television station WABC-TV in New York City, uncovered similar deplorable conditions, including physical and sexual abuse of residents by members of the school's staff. His story aired as "Willowbrook: The Last Disgrace."

A class-action lawsuit was filed against the State of New York in federal court on March 17, 1972. A settlement in the case was reached on May 5, 1975, mandating reforms at the site. Publicity of this case led to the passage of a federal law, "Civil Rights of Institutionalized Persons Act of 1980." In 1983, the State of New York announced plans to close Willowbrook, which had been renamed the Staten Island Developmental Center in 1974.

Whittingham Hospital

Built in 1869 in Lancashire, the now-decaying Whittingham Asylum was at one time the largest of its kind in Britain — it once housed 3,533 patients and 548 staff. This facility boasted its own farms, telephone service, post office, as well as train station, but its biggest claim to fame is as the location that pioneered the use of EEG, the recording of the brain's electrical activity. Much later, allegations of abuse against patients in Whittingham also led to a public outrage, and so staff was dismissed. Patients were relocated during the 1970s and 1980s, and the hospital closed in 1995, with the site derelict and plans for its redevelopment.

Worcester State Hospital

At one time the Bloomingdale Asylum was the primary hospital for mental patients. Located on Belmont Street, construction began in 1833; however, it was the Worcester Lunatic Asylum, built with the Kirkbride Plan design on a location nearby, that took over as the primary facility, as the Bloomingdale Asylum was filled beyond its ability to care for them. The Worcester officially opened its doors in 1879, at a cost more than a million dollars.

The Worcester Insane Asylum was the first of its kind constructed in the state of Massachusetts. This flagstone and brick building stood four stories tall and between the 500-foot wings stood a clock tower, high above the administration building. Interestingly, Sigmund Freud visited the hospital in 1909 during his only trip to America.

In 1991, a massive fire engulfed the Kirkbride building, destroying almost all of the roof and floors, the right most wing, and the administration building. The asylum officially closed in 1991, though operations continued at the facility in a newer building.

In 2004, there was a proposal to build a new facility at this location and replace everything with state-of-the-art equipment and materials. In 2008, there were plans to film *Shutter Island* at this location, but because of the pending demolition of the facility, filming was not approved. Instead, filming took place at Medfield State Hospital.

Worcester State Hospital.
Courtesy of Nan Guzauski.

The remaining Kirkbride wing at
Worcester State Hospital.
Courtesy of Wayne Overla.

Patient room, Worcester State Hospital.
Courtesy of Nan Guzauski.

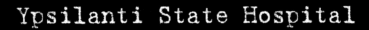

Ypsilanti State Hospital

Ypsilanti State Hospital was a hospital that treated the criminally insane, located in Willis, Michigan. By the end of World War Two, the Ypsilanti State Hospital had two new wards that housed well over 4,000 patients.

In 1959, there were three patients who became quite famous. All three of them believed they were Jesus, and were called The Three Christs of Ypsilanti. For two years, Milton Rokeach, a social psychologist and psychiatrist, spent many, many hours trying to figure out why they believed they were God. The doctor decided to try group therapy with three patients who all had delusions of being Jesus Christ. The logical contradiction of having two other Christs in the room wasn't enough to cure the patients. Rokeech's book, *The Three Christs of Ypsilanti*, became required reading in many psychology classes for years. Despite the doctor's best efforts, he never found out the cause of the three men's delusions and eventually they died at the institution.

Other patients were experimented on by use of drugs. In 1937, two "shock" therapies, using both insulin and Metrazol, induced seizures so severe that patients very often suffered from a fractured spine! The post-World War Two era saw the creation of a substance referred to as L.S.D. CID #527, by the famous Dr. Jonas Salk, which would later lead him to develop the polio vaccine by testing flu vaccines in Ypsilanti State Hospital on what even a U.S. military medical historian loosely describes as "volunteers." The hospital used a judgment call on the unruly patients and how to control them. The suicidal or combative were taken, and out of all sixty-five lobotomy patients in 1953, five died; only one-third improved enough to leave the hospital, according to a member of the hospital staff. Finally, during the Great Depression, the Ypsilanti Savings Bank foreclosed on the property.

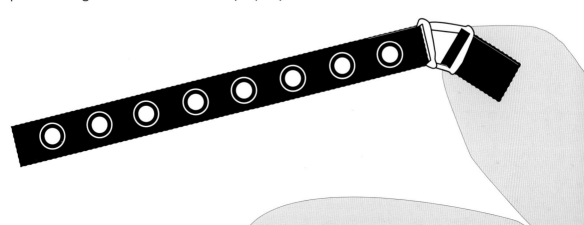

Afterword

Vine Central State Hospital. *Courtesy Chandra Lampriech.*

As far back in time as the Ancient Egyptians, a document known as the "Ebers," written on papyrus, appeared to describe what best can be translated as "disordered states of concentration and attention, and emotional distress in the heart or one's mind" and mentioned how such things were typically treated by reciting magical spells as part of healing rituals. As advanced as we feel we are in the modern world, we have had many pitfalls and mistakes made in how we view and deal with issues we face. It is interesting to me that a few individuals in other eras possess greater wisdom that was later forgotten or ignored. I think to myself how different would things have been if the medical profession would have heeded the wisdom of the great philosopher Aristotle, who abandoned the theory of the divine being the cause of mental illness, and instead proposed that it was caused by physical problems.

The physician Celsus argued that insanity is really present when a continuous dementia begins due to the mind being at the mercy of imaginings. He felt people must heal their own souls through philosophy and personal strength. He described common practices of dietetics, bloodletting, drugs, and counseling — as he called it, "talking therapy" — and he used incantations and magic charms. As time wound its way forward, less emphasis was placed on therapy and attempting to get through to people in a humane way, and instead became as bad as what we see in the best horror films.

As society became more and more "civilized" during the Industrial Revolution and throughout the Victorian Era, the tragedy of our world's history continued. The restraints used and the physical torture utilized to restore control is reminiscent of the Great Inquisition of Europe. Masked and white-gowned jailers dragged terrified and often screaming patients from their cells to an operating room, where various bits of their anatomy were surgically removed. This twisted practice did not end until the advent of chemical straightjackets and public outcry for more humane treatment.

I reflect about these places and the stories of them being haunted. Some believe it to be so; others disagree, saying we create such things. Is it possible we consciously and subconsciously manifest this notion, reinforced by our minds having an instinctual fear of the unknown? Man still carries with him a primal fear, and in places like these, where often the stench of death from the animals that sometimes find their way in the buildings and perish mix with the excitement of the hellish histories of unfathomable misery, it could be simply the power of suggestion that ghosts roam these corridors with us. When the curious venture into these buildings full of moldy and rusting remains, they find nature slowly taking back its place through the very foundation these uninhabited structures, an eerie juxtaposition of familiar combinations makes for the reminder that nothing is forever.

Times have changed, and even though a great deal of the methodology and stereotyping of the mentally ill has improved, it has been only in small increments. Patients were and are still often mistreated, abused and neglected, even if not so cruelly as in the past. Despite significant improvements, the echo of the past's stark realities will haunt us and can only permanently be banished when patients with mental problems are viewed not as dangerous misfits but as real people who once may have had lives, careers, and dreams. So, now you, my reader happen to be left with the ultimate question: Did all of the combined events detailed here over decades leave residual emotional energy in the form of paranormal hauntings? Perhaps it did, but for the poor souls who lived their lives until death came to claim them the reality was far more terrifying than what people claim to have felt when visiting the halls of the ruins we have explored together.

Photo courtesy Dawid Jaguiak.

Bibliography / Sources / Recommended Reading

Anderson, Katherine. *Behind the Walls: Shadows of New England's Asylums*. Self-published, 2009.

Fenna, Kelly. "Fury at 'Village of the Damned' slur." *New York Daily Post*, October 27, 2008.

Mark, Mary Ellen and Karen Folger Jacobs. *Ward 81*. Bolonga, Italy: Damiani, 2008.

Mehr, Joseph, Ph.D. *Illinois Public Mental Health Services: An Illustrated History, 1847-2000*. Ilford, United Kingdom: J. Publishing, 2005.

Michael, Pamela. *Care and Treatment of the Mentally Ill in North Wales, 1800-2000*. United Kingdom: University of Wales Press, 2003.

Scull, Andrew. *Madhouse: A Tragic Tale of Megalomania and Modern Medicine*. New Haven, Connecticut: Yale University Press; 1st edition, April 10, 2005.

Shanahan, Ed. "If the Manteno Walls Could Talk… The Unexplained World — Manteno State." Web: www.Hospitaltheunexplainedworld.com/manteno/

Shaw, Tim. *Haunted Buffalo*. Atglen, Pennsylvania: Schiffer Publishing, Ltd., 2011.

Yanni, Carla. *The Architecture of Madness: Insane Asylums in the United States*. Minneapolis, Minnesota: University of Minnesota Press; 1st edition, 2007.